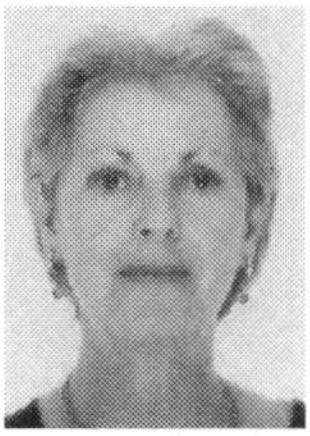

ANGELA LORD is a painter, interior colour designer, muralist and art educator. Born in Christchurch, New Zealand, she studied with Gerard Wagner at the Goetheanum Painting School in Dornach, Switzerland. She founded the Columbine Art Academy in Sussex and London, which offers a diploma recognized by the Arts Section at the Goetheanum, and she teaches around the world, most recently in China and Beirut. Her publications include *The Archetypal Plant: Rudolf Steiner's Watercolour Painting*; *Easter: Rudolf Steiner's Watercolour Painting*; *New Life—Mother and Child, Rudolf Steiner's Madonna Painting*; *Colour Dynamics*, and three books on Creative Form Drawing.

I0803763

Art, Aesthetics and Colour

Aristotle—Thomas Aquinas—Rudolf Steiner

An Anthology of Original Texts

Edited by Angela Lord

TEMPLE LODGE

Temple Lodge Publishing Ltd.
Hillside House, The Square
Forest Row, RH18 5ES

www.templelodge.com

First published by Temple Lodge Publishing 2018

A CIP catalogue record for this book is available from the British Library

ISBN 978 1 912230 22 8

Cover by Morgan Creative
Typeset by DP Photosetting, Neath
Printed and bound by 4Edge Ltd., Essex

Contents

Introduction

In compiling this book, I have endeavoured to place together insights and commentaries on art, aesthetics and colour, which have been bequeathed to western culture by three of its greatest thinkers: Aristotle, Thomas Aquinas and Rudolf Steiner. I have intended to provide a comparative survey, showing how each of these outstanding philosophers employed a unique approach, developed and defined by his own exceptional individuality. I have also indicated the important and significant overlaps in their perceptions, for there are remarkable threads and similarities weaving through their work, which deserve our deeper consideration.

The commentaries of Thomas Aquinas on Aristotle have long been thoroughly researched, documented and widely acknowledged. Rudolf Steiner's insights and public research within this particular stream rest largely upon three lectures which he gave on Thomas Aquinas in 1920, and in just a few references to Aristotle's Categories (see: references and suggested reading). All three philosophers were innovative; all were well in advance of their time, and of their contemporaries; all upheld a seemingly inextinguishable striving for penetrative and truthful understanding. All were deeply concerned with the well-being of humanity; the moral health of society; for the development of human intelligence, and for the spiritual evolution of the world. The expression 'none but himself could be his parallel'—'*palman qui meruit ferat*'—seems to apply to each of them.

My choice of art, aesthetics and colour as themes, is based upon my lifelong love of the arts, and my concern for our contemporary 'thinness' of artistic appreciation, in the classical sense. By selecting and extracting specific quotes from these three thinkers, and arranging them in particular sequences, my intention is to bring an invigorating and refreshing look at a particular historically-related stream of thought, which has contributed significantly to the philosophy of beauty and art. The rich intellectual and spiritual substance created by Aristotle, Thomas Aquinas and Rudolf Steiner has provided an important foundation for the Arts, and for artistic appreciation, relevant in our time and for the future. I would point out that not all three of these great philosophers dealt with each theme as such. Aristotle researched colour phenomena as part of his natural scientific inquiries, but did not apply his colour-research into the field of visual arts. As far as colour was concerned, Aristotle regarded the visual arts as we refer to them today, as a digression, and subject to personal, subjective interpretations, which he was eager to avoid. When he did engage with the 'pure' Arts, he was more concerned with Poetics, Recitation and Drama. Thomas Aquinas regarded the Arts, and the whole question of aesthetics, to be intrinsically bound up with the highest expression of the Divine in human endeavours. As God creates, so could the Divine be revealed in human creativity wrought by Man. For Aquinas, Art was intrinsically bound up with the reason for creating something. For him, for example, logic was one of the highest arts—the beautiful and meaningful order, or sequence, of thought. Art did not even need to reveal itself as an object, or 'thing'; pure metaphysics was an Art, and its reason was to reveal Divine thought in the mind of man. Rudolf Steiner provided many practical examples in all of the Arts, based on his spiritual perceptions. He laid down the basis for an artistic-cultural renewal inspired by, and in order to develop, the faculties of imagination, inspiration and intuition. He brought a new artistic approach into everyday life, into education, architecture, sculpture, painting and into the performing arts, with the intention of re-uniting the Arts with their spiritual source. Realizing that western culture was too much influenced by materialism, he wished to build a bridge between the sense-world and the spiritual-world by utilizing genuine creativity in the Arts.

I am hoping that this book will enable the works of Aristotle and Thomas Aquinas to be enlivened and re-interpreted in the light of Rudolf Steiner's Spiritual Science, and that it will extend their application more widely, rather than their remaining mainly within the areas of theological and academic interpretation.

I hope, also, that it will stimulate a renewed awareness of the need for the pursuit of truth, beauty and knowledge within the Arts and within artistic activity, giving support and providing insights to encourage new, healthier and enlivening artistic expression in our present time.

Angela Lord

Chapter One

Biographies

Aristotle:
Greek philosopher; pupil of Plato; tutor of Alexander the Great; author of works on logic, philosophy, natural science, ethics, politics and poetics. Foremost natural philosopher in the ancient world.

Saint Thomas Aquinas:
Italian Dominican monk, philosopher and theologian.

Rudolf Steiner:
Austrian social philosopher; founder of anthroposophy, or spiritual science.

Aristotle: 384–322 BC*

Aristotle employed a naturalistic, phenomenological outlook, with observations directed towards the outer world. He wished to find out all that could be known about the natural world, forming the fountainhead of modern scientific thought. Through Aristotle's work, Western philosophers were liberated to examine and study the natural world, as well as the ideal. In the Academy in Athens, his teacher Plato gave special attention to politics and legislation, while in the pure scientific field, mathematics and astronomy occupied the main places on the Academy's syllabus. The gifted Aristotle made a great impression on his teacher.

In his way Aristotle was a religious person, but he held that the Divine in the universe is pure intelligence, so that the highest activity for human beings is intellectual activity—reasoning about the world, and striving to understand the world.

He placed a high regard on the input and reliability of the senses of sight, smell, taste, touch and hearing. The shifting images of light, cloud, and water in his Greek homeland were also the inspiration for observations concerning the nature of matter, its transmutations, its powers, its qualities. To him, the changing four seasons of the year displayed seasonal transformations. Alterations in plants, animals and human beings revealed the processes and influences of time, of climate, of environment. Every entity and every event was defined in such a way as to show its particular characteristics. His objective and all-embracing views were organized and categorized into over 700,000 words of commentaries.

In spite of some errors, which are attributable to the limitations of Greek knowledge in the third century BC (or the world-view of his time), he founded the method and the description of nature that is science, and which was to exert an influence for 2,000 years.

In his writing on colour, we can see that his conceptual misunderstandings of certain processes (for example: photosynthesis; the process of ageing; the process of nourishment), led him to mistaken conclusions. His attempts to grasp these processes, and to formulate logical insights are nevertheless the foundations upon which impersonal, objective natural science has been built. One can see an early pathway

* From *American Heritage Dictionary of the English Language* (Houghton Mifflin Company).

being forged, which would be furthered in time by thinkers as diverse as Galileo Galilei, Leonardo da Vinci, Isaac Newton and J. W. Goethe.

His themes and investigations covered fields as diverse as: astronomy and meteorology; animals; botany; marine biology; mineralogy; studies on the human being, including physiology, psychology, social and political issues; ethics; metaphysics; poetry; rhetoric; logic.

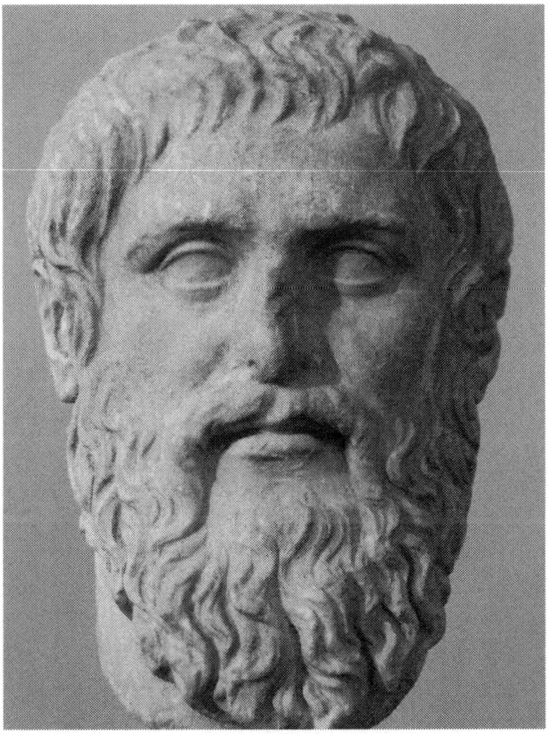

1. Plato, Roman copy of a portrait bust by Silanion for the Academia in Athens (c. 370 BC)

Aristotle—Summary of his Life

384 BC

Born at Stagira, in Chalcidice, Macedonia, on the Aegean Sea. His father, Nicomachus, was physician to the Macedonian King, Amyntas II, grandfather of Alexander the Great. Brought up by his brother-in-law. Taught medicine by his father.

367 BC

At 17 years of age, went to Athens to study at Plato's Academy. Spent 20 years with Plato (427–347 BC). Called 'The intellect of the School'.

374–344 BC
Lived in Assos, on Ionian Coast (East Turkey). Met Theophrastus. Established a branch of the Academy. Married Pythias, who died giving birth to a child also called Pythias. Later lived with Herpyllis of Stagira, who bore his son, Nicomachus.

344–342 BC
Settled at Mytilene, on the island of Lesbos, where he studied marine biology and allied sciences.

342 BC
Returned to Macedonia to tutor the son of King Philip, Alexander (later, Alexander the Great), who was 13 years old. Taught him politics and rhetoric; influenced Alexander's mental and spiritual outlook. Wrote *On Kingship* and *On Colonies*.

340 BC
Returned to Stagira.

336 BC
Athens. He established the Lyceum, which came to be known as the Peripatetic School, a reference to their habit of walking whilst conversing. He collected manuscripts and maps, organized research; inspired his students in many subjects.

335 BC
Began assembling material for an organized encyclopaedia of knowledge. Wrote down his lectures in book form.

323 BC
Fled Athens because of his Macedonian sympathies. Went to island of Euboea where he had property.

322 BC
Died at Chalcis, main city of Euboea.

322 BC
After his death, his friend and successor at the Lyceum, Theophrastus, continued his work, notably on plants.
The Lyceum was destroyed by the Roman General Sulla. Other centres were later closed down by Christian emperors in 86 BC.

And later:

Second century AD
His work on Medicine continued by Galen in Greece; Cosmology and Astronomy by Ptolemy in Alexandria.

Eighth and ninth centuries
Aristotle's and other Greek scientists' work translated into Syriac.

Ninth and tenth centuries
His works translated into Arabic. To the Arab world, Aristotle's work became the foundation of all natural knowledge.

Eleventh and twelfth centuries
Arab scholars in the tradition of Aristotle included: Avicenna (980–1037) in Iran; Averroes (1123–1198) in Spain and Morocco. Centres included Baghdad, Damascus, Cairo and Córdoba.

Twelfth and thirteenth centuries
Aristotle's work spread from Muslim Spain into Central Christian Europe. Translated into Latin.

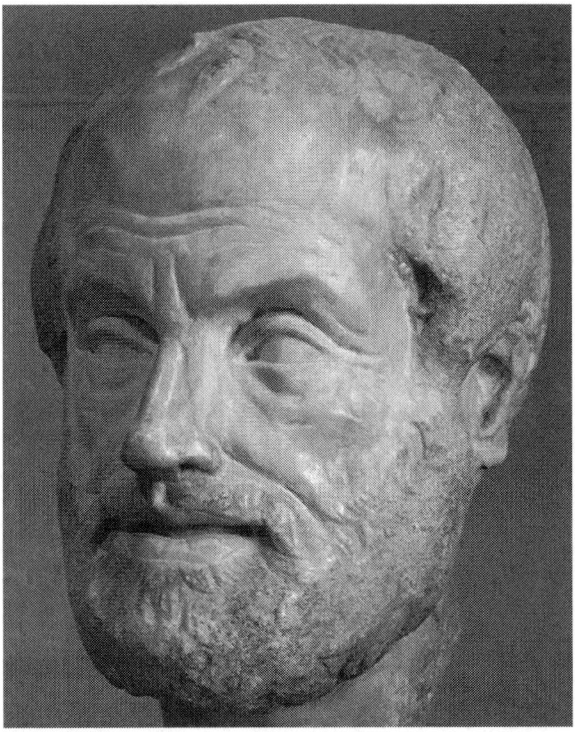

2. Aristotle, Roman copy (1st or 2nd century AD) of a lost bronze sculpture made by Lysippos

Thomas Aquinas: 1225–1274

It was the inspired task of Thomas Aquinas to reconcile the pre-Christian philosophy of Aristotle with Christian theological beliefs. This fusion of the Aristotelian world-picture with Christian ideology, ensured that science and religious faith were able to be compatibly supportive and mutually enriching. Both reason and spiritual revelation were considered to be equally valid, inspired intellectual attributes, and both were needed in the forwarding of Western cultural development.

Some aspects of Thomas Aquinas' philosophy can be seen as a reworking of Aristotelianism, with significant influences from Stoicism, Neoplatonism, Augustinism and Boethianism. It reflects some of the thinking of the Greek commentators on Aristotle, and of Cicero, Plotinus, Avicenna, Averroes, Scotus Eriugena and of his own teacher, Albertus Magnus.

The processes, methods and rigorous discipline which Aristotle developed in his thinking, and in his striving for objectivity, can be observed in the similar mental activity and uncompromising exactitude employed by Thomas Aquinas. Whereas Aristotle directed his intellectual prowess towards the definition of naturalistic, ethical, social and philosophical themes, Thomas Aquinas forged a direct path into a metaphysical, religious sphere. Aristotle formulated observations and commentaries on essence and substance: what a being is. Thomas Aquinas' metaphysical thinking explored the *activity* of being, and sought to define states of existence. Fundamental to Aquinas' metaphysical thinking is the difference between *what* a being is and the reality, or fact, *that* it is.

An inspired theologian, he was acknowledged for divine, or supernatural spiritual revelation, and saw philosophy as a sacred doctrine.

His writings, in Latin, were produced during his 20 years as an active teacher (1252–1273). They consist of several large theological treatises; disputations on theological and philosophical problems; commentaries on several books of the Bible; commentaries on 12 treatises of Aristotle; and many notes, letters, sermons and treatises on philosophical, religious and metaphysical subjects.

He introduced new methods of reasoning about problems, developing his teaching in new and innovative ways. He devoted much thought to the questions: 'What does it mean to be?' and 'How can states of existence be investigated and understood?'

For Thomas Aquinas, metaphysics was the effort to understand reality in general, to find an ultimate explanation of the manifestations of existence through thought. He mentally viewed God, and manifestations of the Spirit, directly and intimately. His own mind sought to understand and to define the mind of God.

The structure of his *Summa Theologica* consists of hundreds of highly specific, detailed questions, with answers, or replies, in compositional debating format. These give expression to his own personal and piercing search for clarity, as well as including counter-arguments, or opposite points of view, which he introduces with the words 'but on the other hand'. This unbiased, magnanimous faculty of reasoning demonstrates his generosity, fairness and flexibility of mind; he reconciles contradictory points of view, and encompasses them with his outstanding intellectual honesty.

In his theory of Art, he is quite intellectualistic, taking Aristotle's Rhetoric, Poetics, and Book VI of *Nicomachean Ethics*, as his major sources. He found an awareness of the spiritual and moral dimensions of the beautiful, found in Dionysius the Areopagite, to develop comments on aesthetics in Aristotle's work. Aquinas considered that Art, and human skill in producing artifacts, shared in the transcendent beauty of God, and that all 'lower' beauties were manifestations of one higher beautiful being (or *pulchritudo*).

The heritage of Aquinas' work has rested largely within the field of Catholic scholarship and within philosophical-theological studies.

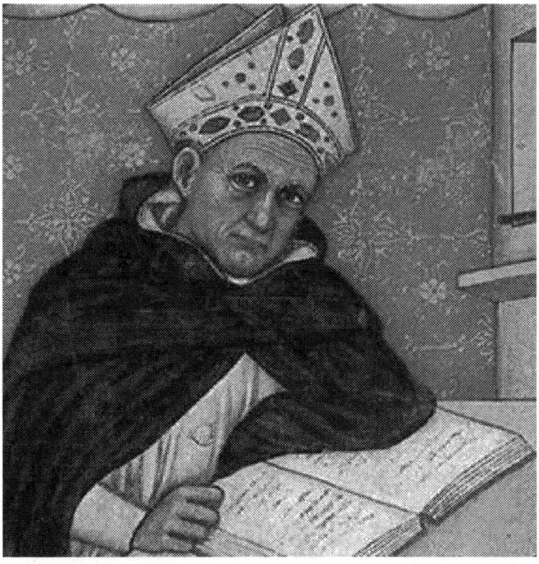

3. St Albertus Magnus by Tommaso da Modena (1352)

Thomas Aquinas—Summary of his Life

1224
Born at Roccasecca, Kingdom of Sicily. Seventh and youngest son of Count Landolfo and Countess Theodora of Aquino. His father was nephew to Emperor Frederick Barbarossa, and was in service to him. His six brothers were all fighting men.

1230
At six years old, began studies under the Benedictine monks at nearby Monte Cassino. Went on to study Liberal Arts at the University of Naples.

1244
Entered the Order of Preachers, the Black Friars (Dominicans). Angered his family. Studied Philosophy and Theology at Dominican Convent in Paris under Albertus Magnus*.

1248
Albertus Magnus called to Cologne, to establish a Dominican College. Took Thomas, his favourite pupil with him.

1252
Thomas sent to University of Paris to advance his studies. Lectured there as a Bachelor in Theology.

1256–1259
Awarded Doctorate in Theology. Became fully accredited member of faculty. Most renowned theological teacher of his time.

1259–1268
Active in various Dominican monasteries near Rome. Extensive study on Aristotle's works. Took up consultative and administrative functions in the Dominican Order.

1269
Second Professorate in Theology at the University in Paris. He had lit-

---

* *Albertus Magnus* (1193–1280):
Called 'doctor universalis'. Theologian of the High Scholastics. Taught at German schools of the Dominican Order, chiefly in Cologne; and at the University of Paris. Studied Alchemy. Chief representative of Aristotelianism among the Scholastics of the thirteenth century.

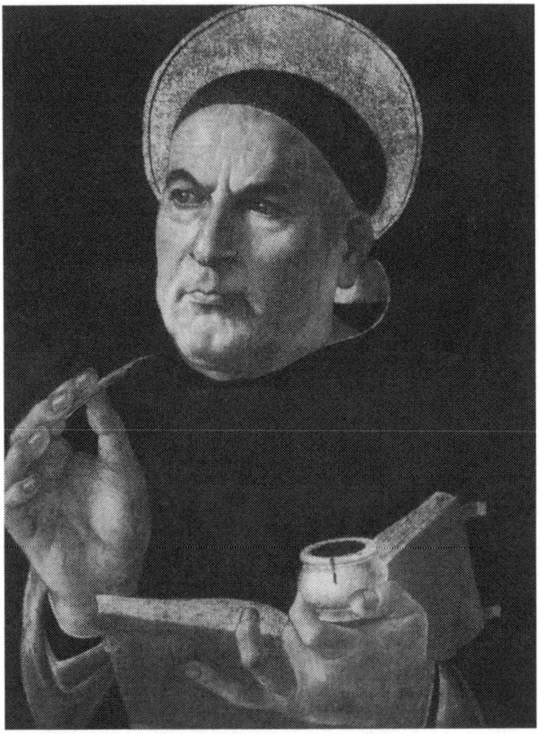

4. St Thomas Aquinas by Sandro Botticelli (1444–1510)

erary works in progress at this time. His innovative methods provoked controversy; had to defend Aristotelianism.

1272
Returned to the Kingdom of Sicily. Taught and preached at the University of Naples.

1273
Illness forced him to discontinue teaching and writing. Whilst celebrating Mass, had a mystical-visionary experience.

1274
Set out to Lyons in France at request of Pope Gregory, to attend church council. Failing health interrupted the trip, not far from his birthplace. Died at Fossanova, at the Cistercian Monastery, in March.

And later:

He was canonized by Pope John XXII in 1323. Declared a Doctor of the Church by Pius V in 1567.

Rudolf Steiner: 1861–1925

Rudolf Steiner called his spiritual philosophy 'Anthroposophy' which is of Greek derivation, meaning 'wisdom (or knowledge) of the Human Being'. His highly developed clairvoyance enabled him to base his work on personal knowledge, and direct perceptions of the spiritual worlds. He developed a modern and universal science of the spirit, which has many relevant and practical applications in fields as diverse as education, agriculture, medicine, social processes, economic principles, the sciences, religion, the visual arts (including architecture), and the performing arts. He also formulated practices of an esoteric training, for meditation and for spiritual development.

Rather than retaining spiritual knowledge within the spheres of the churches, occult movements or spiritual brotherhoods, Rudolf Steiner 'opened-up' esoterically based knowledge for the public. He revealed aspects of cosmic and world evolution; the true nature of the human being; reincarnation and karma.

He wrote and published over 30 books and gave over 6,000 lectures across Europe (later compiled and published), inspiring his readers and audiences, answering their many questions, and providing insights and solutions to many of the world's problems.

He established a centre for Anthroposophy in Switzerland, in Dornach, near Basle. The building, named the Goetheanum (after Johannes Wolfgang von Goethe), holds many conferences throughout the year, has one of Europe's most outstanding theatres and provides studies in all aspects of Anthroposophy.

Rudolf Steiner's concern for the arts was central to his teachings. He attributed the rise in materialism, social problems, and even crime, to the decline in true artistic substance and creativity. He saw the arts as being fundamental to the changes needed in furthering Western cultural life, from tendencies based on a materialistic conception of the world, to impulses and initiatives based on a spiritual world-conception. He ascertained that Art has the capacity to heal, and that artistic activities can enable the human being (at all stages, and from all walks of life), to reach a higher potential. He saw the arts as being the instrument for spiritual revelation, as well as for balancing and harmonizing human nature. His lectures on the arts, and colour, explain the relationship between the spiritual worlds and the material-sense world, offering suggestions and insights for professions in a variety of fields including pedagogical; therapeutic, social, scientific, artistic and philosophical.

The fruits of his work are found in the many 'daughter' movements or offsprings of Anthroposophy, throughout the world. Biodynamic farms; the Camphill Communities (for special needs education and care); Waldorf Schools; therapeutic artistic trainings; the Christian Community Church; drama theatre companies; eurythmy; architectural and design practices; publishing companies; Dr Hauschka and Weleda medicines and cosmetics; hospitals and medical centres; ethical banking and investment businesses, include the many outcomes or branches of his humanitarian-oriented philosophy.

Central to his outlook was the realization that the activity of thinking needed to be redefined and renewed, to include the higher faculties of intuitive insights and perceptions. He saw the development of the human being in the light of world evolution—that our present stage of consciousness is oriented towards materialism, with the external technology of our civilization being produced by means of the intellect, through the concepts of modern science. Rudolf Steiner saw this as having a devas-

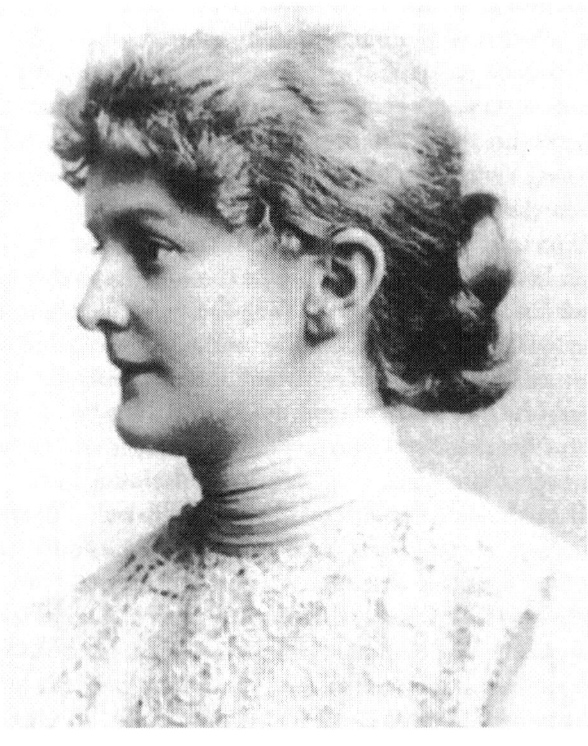

5. Marie Steiner-von Sivers (1903)

tating effect upon spiritual development and considered the future healthy process of world evolution being dependent upon thinking being united with spiritual wisdom.

> However, the nature of humanity is such that when we imbue our thoughts with life—with a spirituality—we send them out into the Cosmos as mirror pictures. All such living thoughts that arise in humanity are seen by the Spiritual Hierarchies glittering back from evolving humanity. And so when human beings are called upon to make their thoughts more alive, they are being called upon to be co-creators with the Divine Beings, for these 'living' thoughts stream out into the Universe as a force for good.
>
> *The Driving Force of Spiritual Powers*, Rudolf Steiner

Rudolf Steiner—Summary of his Life

1861
Born 27 February in Kraljevec (formerly Austro Hungarian Empire, now Croatia) to Austrian parents. His father was an official in the Austrian Southern Railway.

1863–1870
Family lived in Pottschach (a small railway station), then Neudörfl an der Leitha, in Burgenland. As a youth he was aware of a super-sensible world.

1872
Attended school in Wiener-Neustadt.

1879
Studied at Vienna Technical University—maths, chemistry, physics, zoology, botany, mineralogy, geology and the classics. Began his work on Goethe. Karl Julius Schröer, a Goethe scholar, was his professor for German Literature.

1888
Lectured in the Goethe Society: 'Goethe as Father of a New Aesthetic'.

1890
Worked in the Goethe Archives in Weimar, recognizing Goethe as a 'kindred spirit'.

1891
Promoted in Rostock as Doctor of Philosophy by Professor Heinrich von Stein.

1892
Dissertation 'Truth and Science' published.

1894
Wrote *The Philosophy of Freedom*. Visited Nietzsche.

1897
Wrote *Goethe's Worldview*. Moved to Berlin. Edited journal *Magazine for Literature*.

1899
Married the widow Anna Eunike.
Lectured as a staff member of a working men's college; and in the Theosophical Library of Count and Countess Brockdorff. Tutored privately in several families.

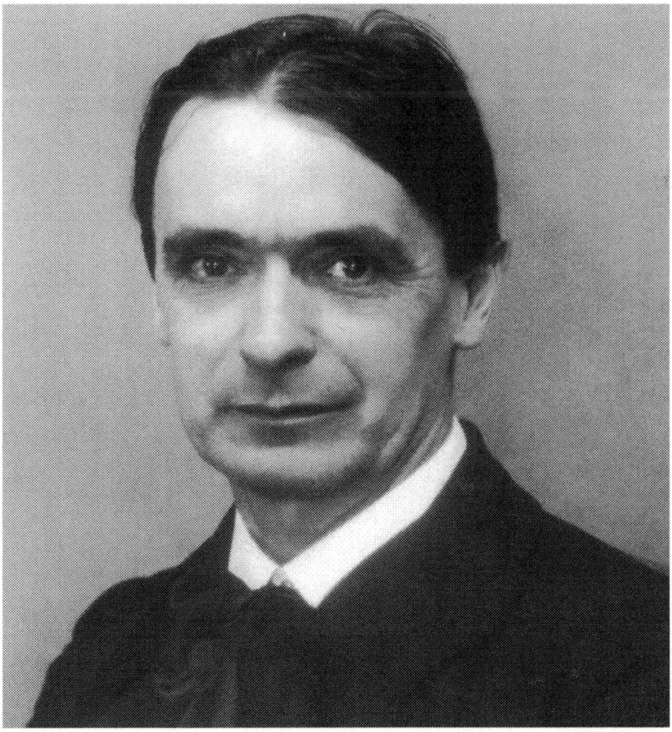

6. Rudolf Steiner

1902
Entered the Theosophical Society.
Wrote *Christianity as a Mystical Fact.*
Began publishing the monthly magazine *Lucifer-Gnosis* with Marie von Sivers.

1903–1912
Lectured widely, including: Berlin, Stuttgart, Munich, Kassel, Hanover, Paris, Basel, Stockholm, Christiania (now Oslo), Florence, Rome, Budapest, Prague, Amsterdam, London.

1909
Met Christian Morgenstern in Berlin.

1911
Anna Steiner-Eunike, his first wife, died.
Throughout this time the development of Anthroposphy was taking place in Munich, through the arts; the Mystery Play performances; Eurythmy. Publishing books and lectures, in Berlin.

1913–1916
Building the first Goetheanum, in Dornach (near Basle). Development of architecture, sculpture, painting. Performances of Mystery Dramas. Tours and lectures throughout central Europe, England, Scandinavia.

1914
Married Marie von Sivers.
Anthroposophical 'headquarters' moved to Switzerland.

1919
Founding of Waldorf School in Stuttgart. Goethe's *Faust* performed in the Goetheanum.

1920–1921
Three lectures on Thomas Aquinas given in Dornach. Continuing courses on natural science, education, medicine, mathematics, astronomy, theology, eurythmy, drama.

1922
Founding of the Christian Community Church.

1922–1923

New Year's Eve. First Goetheanum destroyed by fire.

1923

Refounding of the Anthroposophical Society; branches developing in Germany, Norway, Switzerland, Great Britain, Holland, Austria, Denmark, Sweden, Italy and Czechoslovakia.
Founding of the School of Spiritual Science.

1923–1924

Further tours giving lectures and courses on all themes, including karma research, painting, Christology, agriculture, the evolution of consciousness.
Building the second Goetheanum begins.

1925

Although seriously ill, he continues to be active, writing 'Letters to Members' until shortly before his death, on 30 March in Dornach.

Chapter Two

Art

1. Human effort to imitate, supplement, alter or counteract the work of nature.
2. The conscious production or arrangement of sounds, colours, forms, movements or other elements in a manner that affects the sense of beauty, specifically the production of the beautiful in a graphic or plastic medium.
3. The product of these activities; human works of beauty, collectively.
4. High quality of conception or execution, as found in works of beauty; aesthetic value.
5. A specific skill in adept performance, conceived as requiring the exercise of intuitive faculties that cannot be learned solely by study.*

Now surely as in intelligent action, so in Nature ...
Intelligent action is for the sake of an end; therefore the nature of things also is so. Thus, if a house, for example, had been a thing made by nature, it would have been made in the same way as it is now by art; and if things made by nature were made also by art, they would come to be in the same way as by nature.—Aristotle

From: *Nicomachean Ethics*, Book III, 'Art and Freedom', Physics II, 8 (199a 12)

In order that a man may make good use of the art he has, he needs a good will, which is perfected by moral virtue. For this reason Aristotle says that there is a virtue for art, namely, a moral virtue, inasmuch as the good use of art requires a moral virtue. Clearly it is through justice, which gives him a right will, that a craftsman is set on doing his work faithfully.—Aquinas

From: *Summa Theologica*, 1a 2æ 57, 3, 'Intellectual Virtues', Article 3. 'Is the Intellectual Habit of Art a Virtue?'

---

* All definitions taken from *The American Heritage Dictionary of the English Language* (Houghton Mifflin Company) and *Pocket Oxford Dictionary*.

Art can be really nothing else than a reflection of what human beings feel in relation to the universe. Of course this is possible at various levels and from various standpoints, but on the whole we can speak of a work of art only when it expresses human feeling in such a way that through it the soul is opened to the secrets of the universe.—Steiner

From: *The Four Seasons and the Archangels*, 'Christmas Imagination', October 1923, Dornach

Aristotle

Aristotle divided the arts into those which *complete* nature and those which *imitate* it. This division enabled him to categorize what we would term 'the fine arts' under the title of 'imitative arts'. He distinguished painting, sculpture and poetry from other arts—not because they tend towards beauty or to express feelings, but because at this time they did indeed imitate or reflect the natural world and all of its events, as well as being seen to having a kinship with the objective creative processes of Nature.

Aristotle's theory on art develops ideas of art as being intelligible, and stemming from a natural theory of freedom. His idea of the artist is that of maker, rather than a creator. Natural ugliness can be transformed into something with artistic value once it has been made mimetic or symbolical by means of art and by the artist's technique. He compares a work of art to an organism, presumably meaning that an artist who employs the rational state of the capacity to make and to create, produces a rational whole, or a complete entity, out of active processes akin to nature's activity of creating and making. In a way, Aristotle perceived that Art imitates Nature not by producing a copy but by encouraging and bringing out the inner capabilities and potentials of the materials on which it works. It imitates Nature's procedures.

His philosophy of art is known through the *Poetics*, and it is here that he distinguishes art from nature. In Section III, 'Standard of Artistic Goodness', he is concerned with the determination of excellence in *techne* (or technique): 'The well-made artistic work requires perfection of form and a sureness of method which will guarantee it to be a satisfactory whole in itself and efficacious in its working or effect. This requires, in turn, that the elements in its composition exhibit symmetry, harmony and definiteness.' (Poetry—Section IV, 'Beauty'.)

Aristotle saw music, painting, sculpture and literature to be imitative of human souls, bodies and actions, and that the concept or category 'Art' covered a wide field of human activity and transformation, including building and medicine. In fact, he referred to knowledge itself as an art: '. . . all arts, i.e. all productive forms of knowledge are potencies; they are originative sources of change in another thing or in the artist himself considered as other'.

In this sense the art of artistic activity was viewed also as being an art in its own right.

'COMING-TO-BE' AND ARTISTIC PRODUCTION

Nature and Art

... The causes concerned in the generation of the works of nature are, as we see, more than one. There is the final cause and there is the motor cause. Now we must decide which of these two causes comes first, which second. Plainly, however, that cause is the first which we call the final one. For this is the Reason, and the Reason forms the starting point, alike in the works of art and in works of nature. For consider how the physician or how the builder sets about his work. He starts by forming for himself a definite picture, in the one case perceptible to mind, in the other to sense, of his end—the physician of health, the builder of a house—and this he holds forward as the reason and explanation of each subsequent step that he takes, and of his acting in this or that way as the case may be. Now in the works of nature the good end and the final cause is still more dominant than in works of art such as these, nor is necessity a factor with the same significance in them all; though almost all writers, while they try to refer their origin to this cause, do so without distinguishing the various senses in which the term necessity is used. For there is absolute necessity, manifested in eternal phenomena; and there is hypothetical necessity, manifested in everything that is generated by nature as in everything that is produced by art, be it a house or what it may. For if a house or other such final object is to be realized, it is necessary that such and such material shall exist; and it is necessary that first this and then that shall be produced, and first this and then that set in motion, and so on in continuous succession, until the end and final result is reached, for the sake of which each prior thing is produced and exists. As with these productions of art, so also is it with the productions of nature.

From *Parts of Animals* ($639^b/640^c$), Book I (639^b 10–30)

For man is generated from man; and thus it is the possession of certain characters by the parent that determines the development of like characters in the child. The same statement holds good also for the operations of art, and even for those which are apparently spontaneous. For the same result as is produced by art may occur spontaneously. Spontaneity, for instance, may bring about the restoration of health. The products of art, however, require the preexistence of an efficient cause homogeneous with themselves, such as the statuary's art, which must necessarily precede the statue; for this cannot possibly be produced spontaneously. Art indeed consists in the conception of the result to be produced before its realization in the material. As with spontaneity, so with chance; for this also produces the same result as art and by the same process.

(640^{c} 20–30)

Of things that come to be, some come to be by nature, some by art, some spontaneously. Now everything that comes to be comes to be by the agency of something and from something and comes to be something. And the something which I say it comes to be may be found in any category; it may come to be either a 'this' or of some size or of some quality or somewhere.

Now natural comings to be are the comings to be of those things which come to be by nature; and that out of which they come to be is what we call matter; and that by which they come to be is something which exists naturally; and the something which they come to be is a man or a plant or one of the things of this kind which we say are substances if anything is—all things produced either by nature or by art have matter; for each of them is capable both of being and of not being, and this capacity is the matter in each—and, in general, both that from which they are produced is nature, and the type according to which they are produced is nature (for that which is produced, e.g. a plant or an animal, has a nature), and so is that by which they are produced—the so-called 'formal' nature, which is specifically the same (though this is in another individual); for man begets man.

Thus, then, are natural products produced; all other productions are called 'makings'. And all makings proceed either from art or from a faculty or from thought. Some of them happen also spontaneously or by luck just as natural products sometimes do; for there also the same things sometimes are produced without seed as well as from seed. Concerning these cases, then, we must inquire later, but from art proceed the things of which the form is in the soul of the artist. (By form I mean the essence of each thing and its primary substance.)

From *Metaphysics* (1032^{a}–1032^{b}), Book VII (1032^{a} 12–30)

For even contraries have in a sense the same form; for the substance of a privation is the opposite substance, e.g. health is the substance of

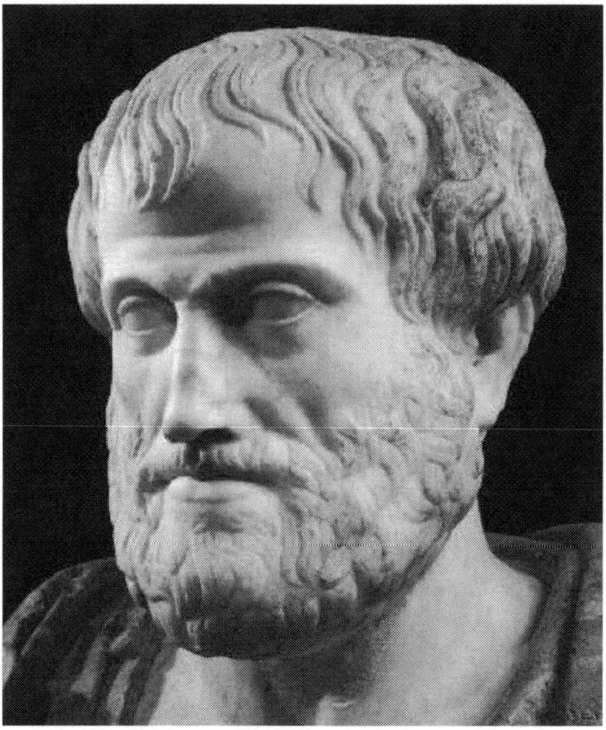

7. *Aristotle*

disease (for disease is the absence of health); and health is the formula in the soul or the knowledge of it. The healthy subject is produced as the result of the following train of thought:—since *this* is health, if the subject is to be healthy *this* must first be present, e.g. a uniform state of body, and if this is to be present, there must be heat; and the physician goes on thinking thus until he reduces the matter to a final something which he himself can produce. Then the process from this point onwards, i.e. the process towards health, is called a 'making'. Therefore it follows that in a sense health comes from health and house from house, that with matter from that without matter; for the medical art and the building art are the form of health and of the house, and when I speak of substance without matter I mean the essence.

Of the productions or processes one part is called thinking and the other making—that which proceeds from the starting point and the form is thinking, and that which proceeds from the final step of the thinking is making.

(1032^b 5–15)

. . . Now since architecture is an art and is essentially a reasoned state of capacity to make, and there is neither any art that is not such a state nor any such state that is not an art, *art* is identical with a state of capacity to make, involving a true course of reasoning. All art is concerned with coming into being, i.e. with contriving and considering how something may come into being which is capable of either being or not being, and whose origin is in the maker and not in the thing made; for art is concerned neither with things that are, or come into being by necessity, nor with things that do so in accordance with nature (since these have their origin in themselves). Making and acting being different, art must be a matter of making, not of acting. And in a sense change and art are concerned with the same objects; as Agathon says, 'art loves chance and chance loves art'. Art, then, as has been said, is a state concerned with making, involving a true course of reasoning, and lack of art on the contrary is a state concerned with making, involving a false course of reasoning; both are concerned with the variable.

From *Nicomachean Ethics* (1140^a), Book VII (1140^a 10–20)

Now intelligent action is for the sake of an end; therefore the nature of things also is so. Thus if a house, for example, had been a thing made by nature, it would have been made in the same way as it is now by art; and if things made by nature were made also by art, they would come to be in the same way as by nature. Each step then in the series is for the sake of the next; and generally art partly completes what nature cannot bring to a finish, and partly imitates her. If, therefore, artificial products are for the sake of an end, so clearly also are natural products.

From *Nicomachean Ethics*, Book III, 'Art and Freedom', Physics, Physics II, 8 (199^a 12–20)

It is absurd to suppose that purpose is not present because we do not observe the agent deliberating. Art does not deliberate. If the shipbuilding art were in the wood, it would produce the same results *by nature*. If, therefore, purpose is present in art, it is present also in nature. The best illustration is a doctor doctoring himself; nature is like that.

(199^b 26–30)

Thomas Aquinas

Following Aristotle's maxim that knowledge presupposes an essential likeness between the knower and thing known, and because human nature is both corporeal and intellectual, Thomas Aquinas held that knowledge necessarily begins with sense perception. This conviction that arguments and definitions must start with facts of the natural world, gave his proofs for the existence of God their characteristic form. He treated sacred doctrine as a single discipline, embracing the whole life of the church, including worship, morals and spiritual practice. Aquinas identified God's image in human beings with their capacity to know and direct their own activity. His moral theology deals firstly with happiness as the end of human existence and then with the soul's faculties and powers, which can be directed by virtue and guided by law and grace as a means to achieving this divinely inspired state of happiness or spiritual fulfilment. The first principles of moral knowledge, the Natural Law, are part of human nature; the law of the Gospel is the grace of the Holy Spirit which transforms and elevates human nature; and Christ's humanity had a causal relationship to the work of redemption. He explored the possibility of furthering the Aristotelian philosophy of substance to develop a systematic understanding of transubstantiation.

He understood Art to be a special habit or acquired skill of the practical intellect, or man's mind applied to problems of activity. He defined prudence as the right reason for doing things ('*recta ratio agibilium*'), which he used in reference to moral discourse. The term 'prudence' (or prudens) is related to provident, or having or showing foresight. It can also mean 'of, or by, divine foresight'. Aquinas defined Art as 'the right reason for making things' ('*recta ratio factibilium*'). The Arts were intrinsically related to the right application of prudence and of virtue.

Some works of art and artifacts he saw as being merely useful, others as beautiful and still others existing only in the ordering of thinking. Here, in this latter aspect Aquinas took seriously that logic is an art.

By 'art', Aquinas is referring not only to a finished work of art, but also to the process of bringing something about. Aquinas speaks of the arts in a broad sense, including the professions of medicine and navigation. Here he uses the term 'art' to imply skill, artistry, proficiency, ability, application, knowledge, craftsmanship or capacity (for example).

He considered the Dominican monastical way of life to be a living work of art. The various aspects and activities of community life formed a spiritually-artistically crafted life, oriented in a rhythmical daily service to God.

It is important to consider that Aristotle's all-embracing view of the arts influenced Thomas Aquinas to the extent that he also considered what we would refer to as skills, professions or vocations, as arts. For example, medicine, farming and education are arts which co-operate with natural evolutionary processes in order to assist and perfect them. Other arts, such as architecture and carpentry adapt and enhance nature's logical processes of operation and technique in order that results can come about which nature could not accomplish. The arts of philosophy and legislation strive to copy or to recreate laws of justice from observation of their eternal paradigms in nature, influenced by the Platonic view of philosophy being an imitative art, making 'copies' of the Ideas of truth. Hence 'art copies nature'.

Both Aristotle and Aquinas made a distinction between the mimetic arts which copy appearances from nature, and utilitarian arts (such as medicine or farming), which assist natural organisms to reach maturity, normality or perfection.

In Aristotle's *Metaphysics* 1034a 8–30, he refers to two kinds of artifice: one in which matter can organize itself towards a required end (e.g. medicine, which directs or corrects a natural organic process); and a second type of artifice in which inert materials are used (such as in architecture). Aquinas also makes the same distinction, in reference to this passage, between the arts which co-operate with nature and employ it as an active principle, and the arts which employ natural material to achieve a result which no natural process could achieve.

CREATION OF THE MATERIAL UNIVERSE

Regarding the work of creation: do material creatures come from God? Article 3: Were the Angels God's intermediaries in making them?

Point 2: God is one and yet has knowledge of different things without this detracting from his simplicity. Thus, through his wisdom, he is also the cause of different things being produced in accordance with the diversity he knows, just as an artist produces different objects of art, after conceiving the ideas for them . . .

. . . Avicenna and certain others maintained that forms found in corporeal things do not subsist separately, but only in some mind. They held that all forms now existing in corporeal matter proceed from forms that exist in the minds of spiritual creatures, which they refer to as 'intelligences', and Christians refer to as Angels; this is similar to the way in which art forms come from forms existing in the mind of the artist . . .

. . . Forms participated in matter are not reducible to unmaterialized forms that serve as patterns, as the Platonists maintained. Rather, they are traceable to mental forms, either those of angelic intellects, whence they proceed through a process of movement, or to ideas in the divine mind, which endowed created things even with the seeds of forms that they might be brought to full realization through a process of movement.

Summa Theologica (Volume 10, 'Cosmogony', 1a. 65–67)

EMANATION OF THINGS

Article 8: Obj. One, 'Whether Creation enters into the works of Nature and Art'

It would seem that creation enters into the works of nature and art. For in every operation of nature and art some form is produced . . . in every operation of nature and art there is creation.

Summa Theologica (1a 2æ. 57, 3), Article 3. 'Is the Intellectual Habit of Art a Virtue?'

The Third Point:

1. It would seem that art is not an intellectual virtue. Augustine, in fact, says that *no one makes bad use of virtue*. One may, however, make bad use of art, for a craftsman can work badly according to the knowledge of his art. Art, therefore, is not a virtue.
2. Furthermore, there is no virtue of a virtue. Now, it is said, a virtue is needed for art. Consequently, art is not a virtue.
3. Moreover, the liberal arts are more excellent than the mechanical arts. Yet just as the mechanical arts are practical, so the liberal arts are speculative. If art were an intellectual virtue, therefore, it would have to be listed among the speculative virtues.

On the Other Hand: Aristotle says that art is a virtue. He does not, however, enumerate it among the speculative virtues which, according to him, reside in the scientific part of the soul.

Reply: Art is nothing other than right judgement about things to be made. Yet the good of these things depends, not upon the disposition of

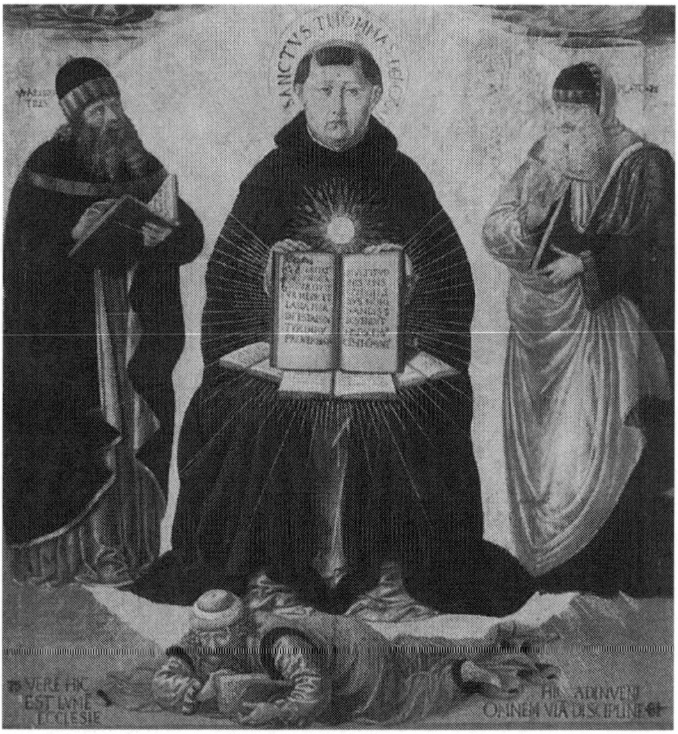

8. 'Triumph of St Thomas Aquinas', between Plato and Aristotle, by Benozzo Gozzoli (1471)

the maker's appetite, but on the worth of the very work done. An artist as such is not commendable for the will with which he makes a work, but for its quality. Art properly speaking is, then, a practical habit.

Yet it has something in common with the speculative habits, since the quality of the things they consider by them is a matter of concern to them, but the moral disposition from which they were produced is not. In fact, so long as a geometrician demonstrates the truth, it does not matter how he feels about it, whether he is joyful or angry; neither, as we have observed, is it relevant to the artist as such. And so, art has the nature of a virtue in the same way as the speculative habits have; namely neither art nor a speculative habit makes a good work with regard to a man's using it well, the habit, which is the distinctive function of a virtue perfecting the appetite. Art, like the speculative habits, gives only the ability to act well.

Hence:

1. When anyone endowed with art produces bad work, this is not the work of his art; but contrary to it: as when, though knowing

the truth, a man lies, his words are contrary to, and not in accord with his knowledge. Accordingly, just as science is always related to good, as stated above, so is art; and it is for this reason that it is called a virtue. Yet it falls short of the notion of perfect virtue, because it does not ensure the good use of what it produces, for which something further is required, although there cannot be a good use without a good art.

2. In order that a man may make good use of the art he has, he needs a good will, which is perfected by moral virtue. For this reason, Aristotle says that there is a virtue for art, namely, a moral virtue, inasmuch as the good use of art requires a moral virtue. Clearly it is through justice, which gives him a right will, that a craftsman is set on doing his work faithfully.
3. Even in speculative matters there is something by way of work, for instance, constructing a syllogism or passage of prose and counting and measuring. Hence whatever habits of the speculative reason are ordained to such works, are by analogy called arts, but liberal arts, in order to show their difference from arts directed to works done by the body, which are, after a fashion, servile, in that the body is a subject in the service of the soul, and man because of his soul, is free, *liber*. Those sciences, on the other hand, which are not ordained to any such work, are called sciences purely and simply, and not arts. Nor, if the liberal arts are nobler, does it follow that the notion of art is more applicable to them.

Article 4, 'Is Prudence a Virtue distinct from art?'

The Fourth Point:

1. It would seem that prudence is not a virtue distinct from art. Art is right reason applied to certain works... Since, therefore, prudence is also right reason about works, it seems that it too should be reckoned an art.
2. Furthermore, prudence has more in common with art than the speculative habits have, since they are both *about contingent matters that may be otherwise than they are*. Some speculative habits, however, are called arts. Much more, therefore, should prudence be called an art.
3. Moreover, it belongs to prudence *to be of good counsel*. Counselling, however, takes place in certain arts also, e.g. in the arts of warfare, of seamanship and of medicine. Prudence, therefore, is not distinct from art.

On the Other Hand: Aristotle distinguishes prudence from art.

Reply: Where you find the nature of virtue is diverse, there you should distinguish between virtues. It has been stated above that some habits fulfil the meaning of virtue merely conferring the capability to do something well, while others not only do this but ensure that it is performed well. Art gives merely the ability, since it does not involve appetite, whereas prudence also provides for the good being executed, since as presupposing right-love,* it involves the appetite.

The reason for the difference is that art is right judgement about things to be produced, while prudence is rectified judgement about things to be done. Producing and doing differ, as stated in the *Metaphysics*, in that producing is an action passing into external matter, thus to build, to saw, and the like; whereas doing is an activity abiding in an agent, thus to see, to will and the like.

. . . The worth of things produced by art, however, does not consist in their being good for human appetite, but in the good of the products of art themselves. Hence art does not presuppose rightness of appetite. As a consequence more praise is given to a craftsman who deliberately violates the rules of his craft than to one who does so unwillingly, whereas a willed mistake is more opposed to prudence than one unwilled, since rightness of will is essential to prudence, but not to act. Accordingly, it is evident that prudence is a virtue distinct from art.

Hence:

1. The various kinds of things made by art are all external to a man, and the meaning of virtue is not thereby diversified. Prudence, however, is right reason in human acts themselves and accordingly is a distinct kind of virtue.
2. Prudence has more in common with art than a speculative habit has, if we consider where they are and what they are about. Both lie in that part of the soul concerned with probabilities, and are concerned in things which may be otherwise than they are. Considered as virtues, however, art has more in common with the speculative habits than with prudence, as appears from what has been said.

* In reference to the goals of human life.

Article 5, 'Is Prudence a Virtue Necessary to a Man?'

1. It would seem that prudence is not a virtue necessary for a good life. For as art is to things to be made, for it puts right reason into them, so is prudence to things to be done, for it is right reason in them: thus the Ethics. Now art is required only for them to be made, not after they have been made. Likewise prudence is not necessary to lead a good life, once a man has become virtuous, but only perhaps in order for him to become virtuous.

Aristotle requires art to be complemented by virtue because of itself it does not imply rightly disposed affection. Hence to use art aright a person must have moral virtue, which straightens out his loves. Yet prudence finds no place in the processes of art itself, both because art is ordered to a restricted end and because it employs determinate methods to achieve it. Nevertheless by analogy you may speak of works of art being done prudently, because with some arts the means to the end allow uncertainty, and need to be deliberated over.

Summa Theologica (2a 2æ 47,4), 'The Nature of Prudence'

The principle (or source) of works of art is the human intellect which is derived by some sort of similitude from the divine intellect, and the latter is the principle of all things in nature. Hence not only must artistic activities imitate nature, but even art products must imitate the things which exist in nature.

1 Politicorum 1

Summa Theologica, Volume 42, 'Courage', Question 134: 'Is Magnificence a Virtue?'

Reply: Art is the right method of making things, as Aristotle puts it. But magnificence, or making great things, is concerned with works to be made, as the word itself indicates. So it is an art, rather than a virtue.

On the Other Hand: Art must have a certain virtue as Aristotle remarks. This is the moral virtue by which the desire may be disposed to make right use of the methods of art. This is the function of magnificence, so it is not an art, it is a virtue.

Rudolf Steiner

At the turn of the twentieth century it was already clear to Rudolf Steiner that the arts were becoming increasingly devoid of spiritually inspired content and direction. This was due to the natural progression of the urge for freedom, and the necessity for artists to gain individuality of expression. A longing to throw off the restrictions and formalities of the past was leading towards an exciting, open field of individual creativity. A breaking down of all the rules and constraints, and an abandoning of hindering traditions gave artists the opportunity to develop new forms of artistic experimentation.

However, this would inevitably lead (on the whole) into superficiality, abstraction and an intellectualization of the arts, and to an inflation of personality.

Rudolf Steiner developed the visual arts of architecture, sculpture and painting in connection to human relationships within society, to the world of the senses, and to the spiritual worlds. The performing arts were to regain dignity, depth and spiritual substance. Artists would bring truth, beauty and goodness to nourish and stimulate an understanding of humanity's divinity, and would, out of newly-developing faculties of artistic perception, be able to give insights to natural world phenomena and to the spiritual nature of world evolution.

Rudolf Steiner regarded the arts as being essential manifestations of the spirit—that the spiritual worlds could be portrayed within physical materials which could reveal the secrets of the universe, of nature and of the human being.

He spoke, in his lectures on Thomas Aquinas:

> Spiritual science is seeking to range itself as a corrective, side by side with Natural Science . . . What we see as Nature can be penetrated as the veil of natural existence. One presses on beyond the limit of knowledge, one penetrates into this material world and discovers that this is in fact the spiritual world, that behind the veil of Nature there are in truth not material atoms, but spiritual beings. This is how progressive thought deals with a continued development of Thomism in the Middle Ages.

The new initiation science which Rudolf Steiner brought, challenges our conceptualized world-view to the extent that we are asked to give art a new orientation, to base it within a spiritual reality, a spiritually-oriented world outlook.

In a lecture on 'Spirit and Non-Spirit in Painting', he spoke:

> The work of art, or creation, to which one gives objective life must be alive in the spiritual atmosphere of the world. If one forgets this spiritual relationship, art goes through a transformation and changes more or less into non-art.
>
> Colours and sounds are windows through which we can ascend spiritually into the spirit world, and life also brings to us windows through which the spiritual world enters our physical world.*

In lectures on Art History, he describes the influences which both sense and super-sensory experiences have on the arts. Each phase of historical cultural development sought for and gave expression to an artistic style appropriate for the consciousness of its time.

Initially, divinely inspired works of art elevated earthly experiences towards heavenly realms.

Gradually, as spiritual perceptions withdrew and influences of the exterior sense-world increased, the individual personality developed.

Imaginations then created reflections of that which clairvoyant consciousness could no longer perceive. It was as though from the Middle Ages and onwards into the Renaissance the arts served as a reflection to inspire, uplift and to remind us of the worlds adjacent to the everyday world of the physical senses worlds which, by then, were becoming increasingly invisible.

Steiner urged that in our present time it is necessary to release art from its conceptual imprisonment within matter, within the constraints of a materialistic world-view, in order that cultural and social life would be able to pursue the highest goals for humanity.

> Art forms a bridge across the abyss. This is why art must realize that its task is to carry the spiritual-divine life into the earthly, to fashion the latter in such a way that its forms, colours, words, tones, act as a revelation of the world beyond. Whether art takes on an idealistic or naturalistic tendency is of no importance. What it needs is a relationship to the truly, not merely thought out, spiritual. No artist could create in his medium if there were not alive in him impulses springing from the spiritual world. This fact points to the seriousness of art, standing alongside the seriousness of cognition and religious experience.

---

* From *Colour.*

'Moral Experience of the Worlds of Colour and Tone', from *The Arts and Their Mission*, Lecture 4, Dornach, 3 June 1923

We must seek to have an inner connection between all our work with forms and colours, and our spiritual knowledge which moves us to the innermost depths of our souls and is alive in us in spirit.... Therefore there must be unity between what there is in man's innermost soul.... Bridges must be built between what are still abstract ideas of Spiritual Science, and what flows from our hands, our chisel, or our brush.

'The Creative World of Colour', from *Colour*, Dornach, 26 July 1914

In all ages the human souls in which the artistic element flourished have had a definite relation to the spiritual world. It was out of a spirit-attuned state that the artistic urge proceeded. And this relation to the spiritual world will be, forever, the prerequisite for genuine creativity. Any age strictly naturalistic must, to be true to itself,

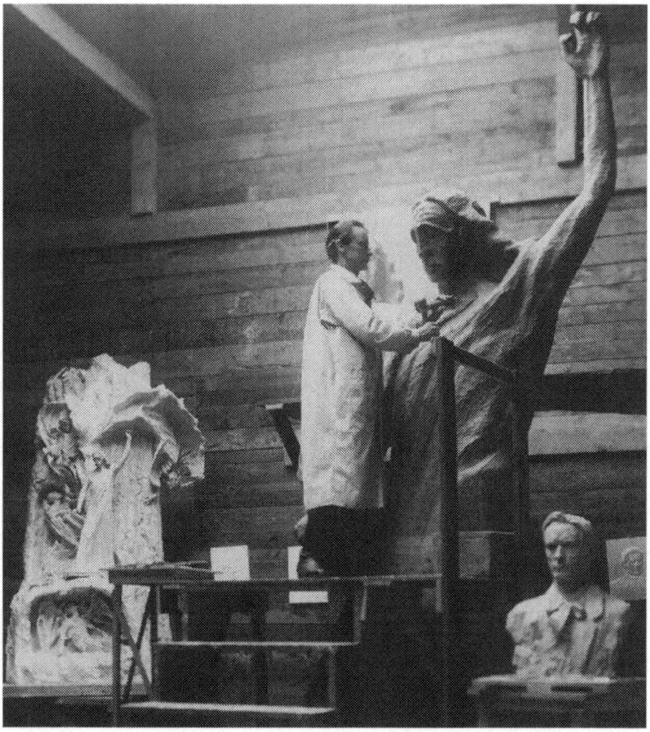

9. Rudolf Steiner working on his sculpture 'The Representative of Humanity' (1919)

become inartistic, philistine. Unfortunately, our own age has an immense talent for philistinism.

The Arts and Their Mission, Lecture 2, Dornach, 1 June 1923

Art is eternal, yet its forms change. And if you realize that art always has a relation to the spirit you will understand that both in creating it and appreciating it, art is something through which one enters the spiritual world. An artist may create a picture in a lonely desert, not worrying about who will look at the picture, or whether anyone at all will look at it. For the artist creates within a divine spiritual community. Gods are looking over the artist's shoulder—he or she is creating in their company.

'Spirit and non-Spirit in Painting', from *The Arts and their Mission*, Dornach, 9 June 1923

Of the revelations through art one thing at least can truly be said: they act upon our soul with powerful conviction and permeate our feelings with a sense of truth, to an extent which renders all logical reasoning and merely rational knowledge powerless ...

... When we confront great works of art in the sense of spiritual science, we feel that the message they convey is another revelation of humanity's search for truth.

'The Mission of Art', 12 May 1910

Art can be really nothing else than a reflection of what human beings feel in relation to the universe. Of course this is possible at various levels and from various standpoints but, on the whole, we can speak of a work of art only when it expresses human feeling in such a way that through it the soul is opened to the secrets of the universe.

'The Christmas Imagination', from *The Four Seasons and the Archangels*, October 1923

Art, always a daughter of the divine, has become estranged from her parent. If art finds its way back to its origins and is, again and again accepted by the divine, then it will become what it should within civilization, within worldwide culture: an endowment of benefit to humanity.

The Arts and Their Mission, Dornach, 9 June 1923

It must become the striving of art to dip down once again into elemental life. Art has looked at and studied nature long enough. It has tried long enough to solve every kind of natural riddle, and to reproduce in works of art in another form what can be seen by means of penetrating nature. What lives in the elements, however, is still something dead for the art of today... A new art will unfold when the human soul learns to immerse itself and to deepen itself in what is elemental and living.

Colour, Dornach, 26 July 1914

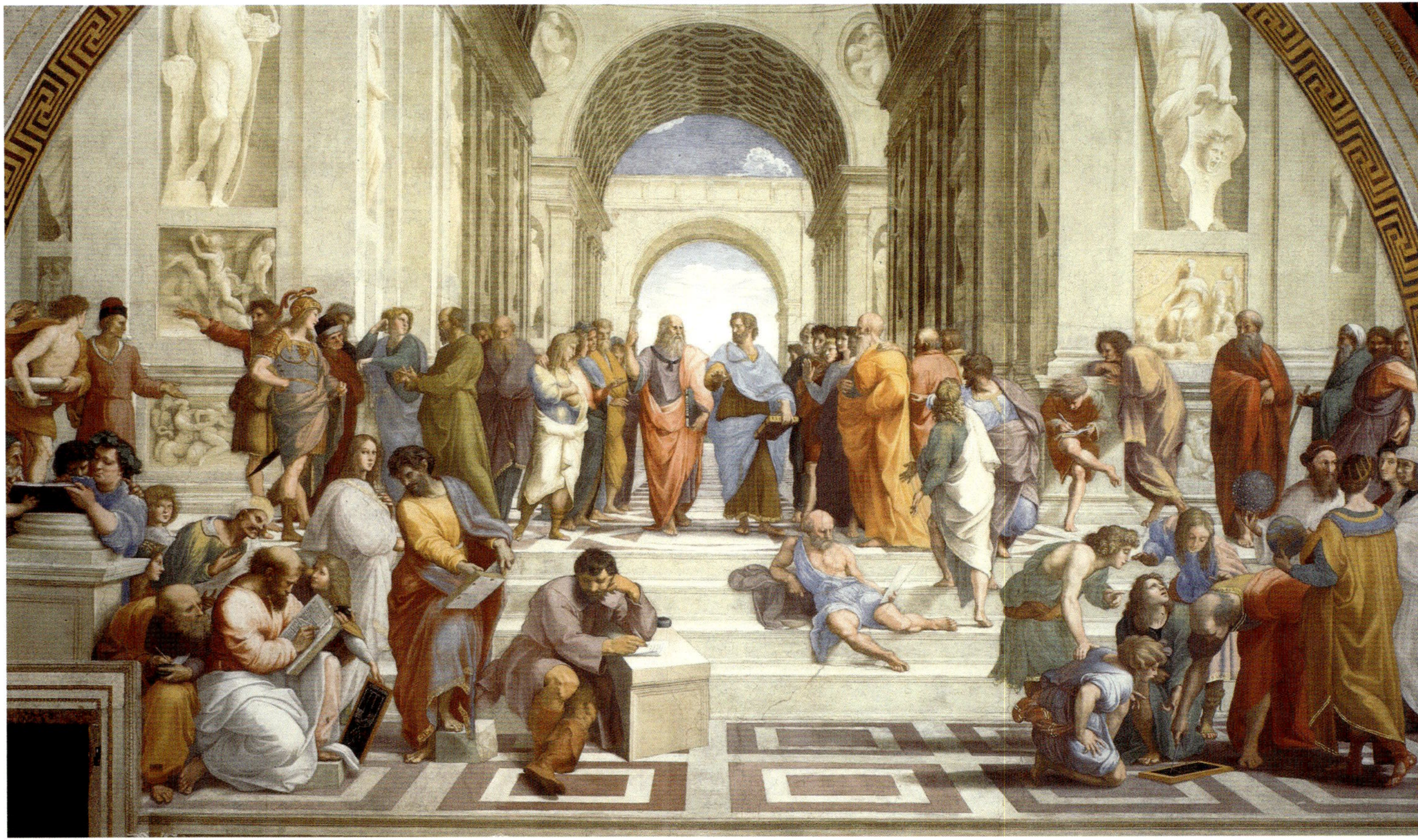

1. *'The School of Athens' by Raphael* (see p. 41). (Painted between 1509 and 1511.)

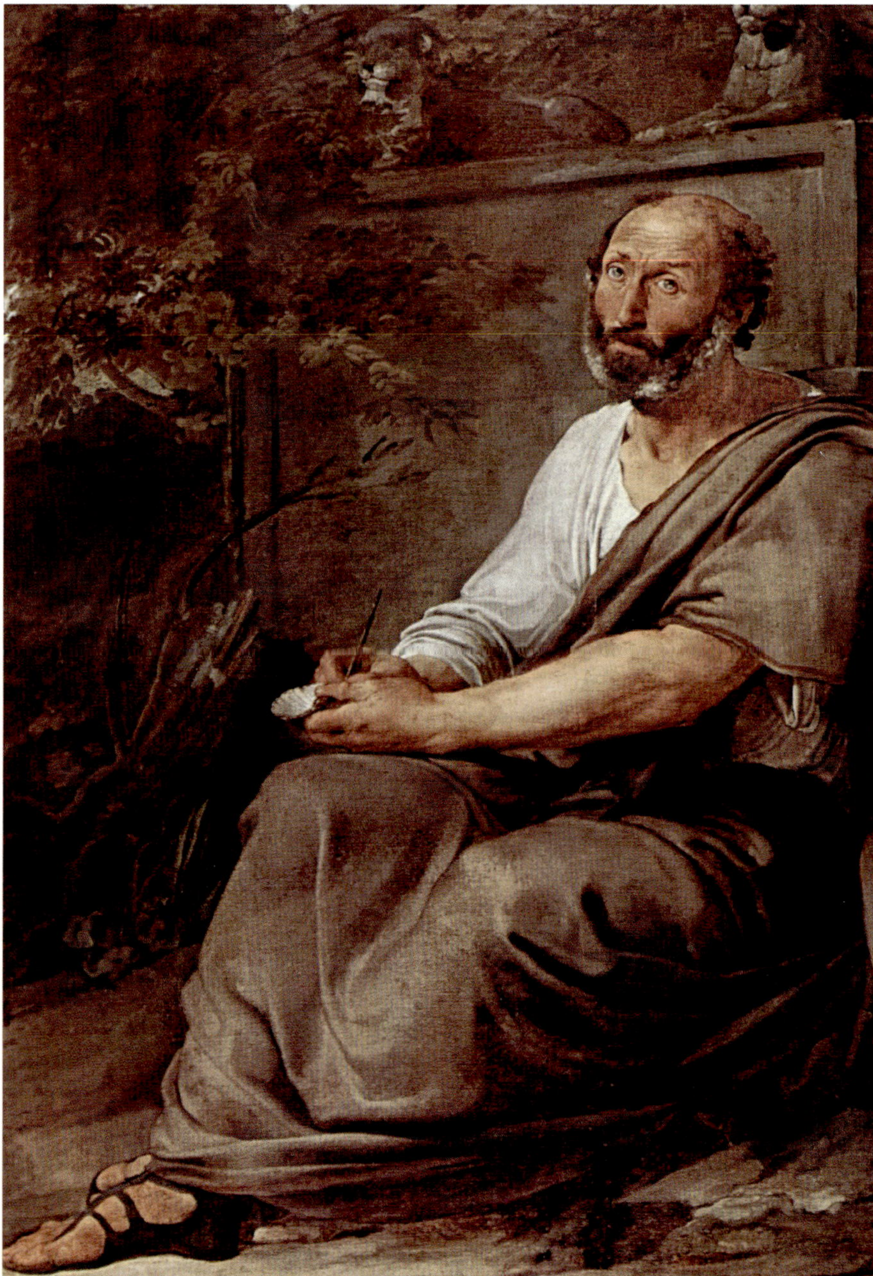

2. *Aristotle by Francesco Hayez (1811)*

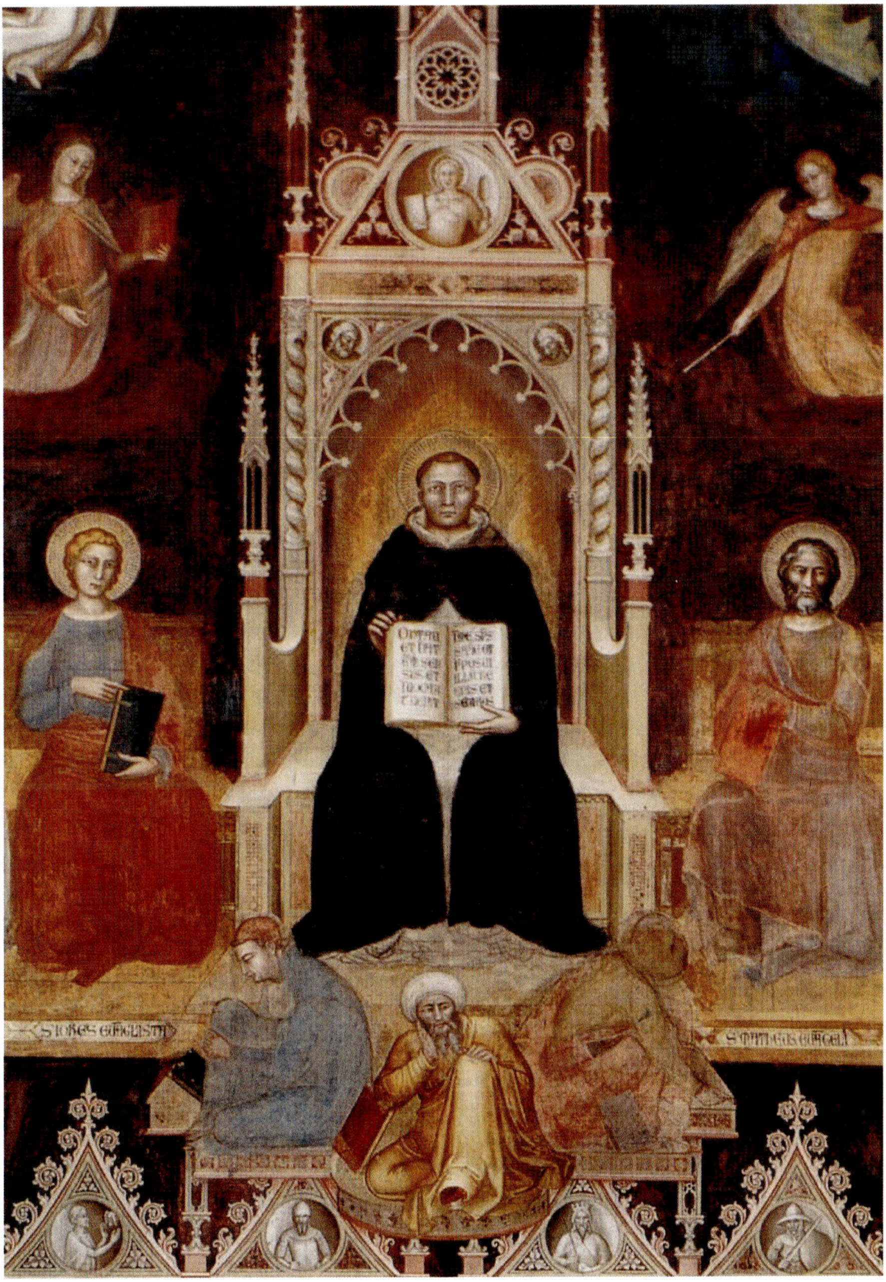

3. *'Triumph of St Thomas Aquinas' by Andrea di Bonaiuto (1366)*

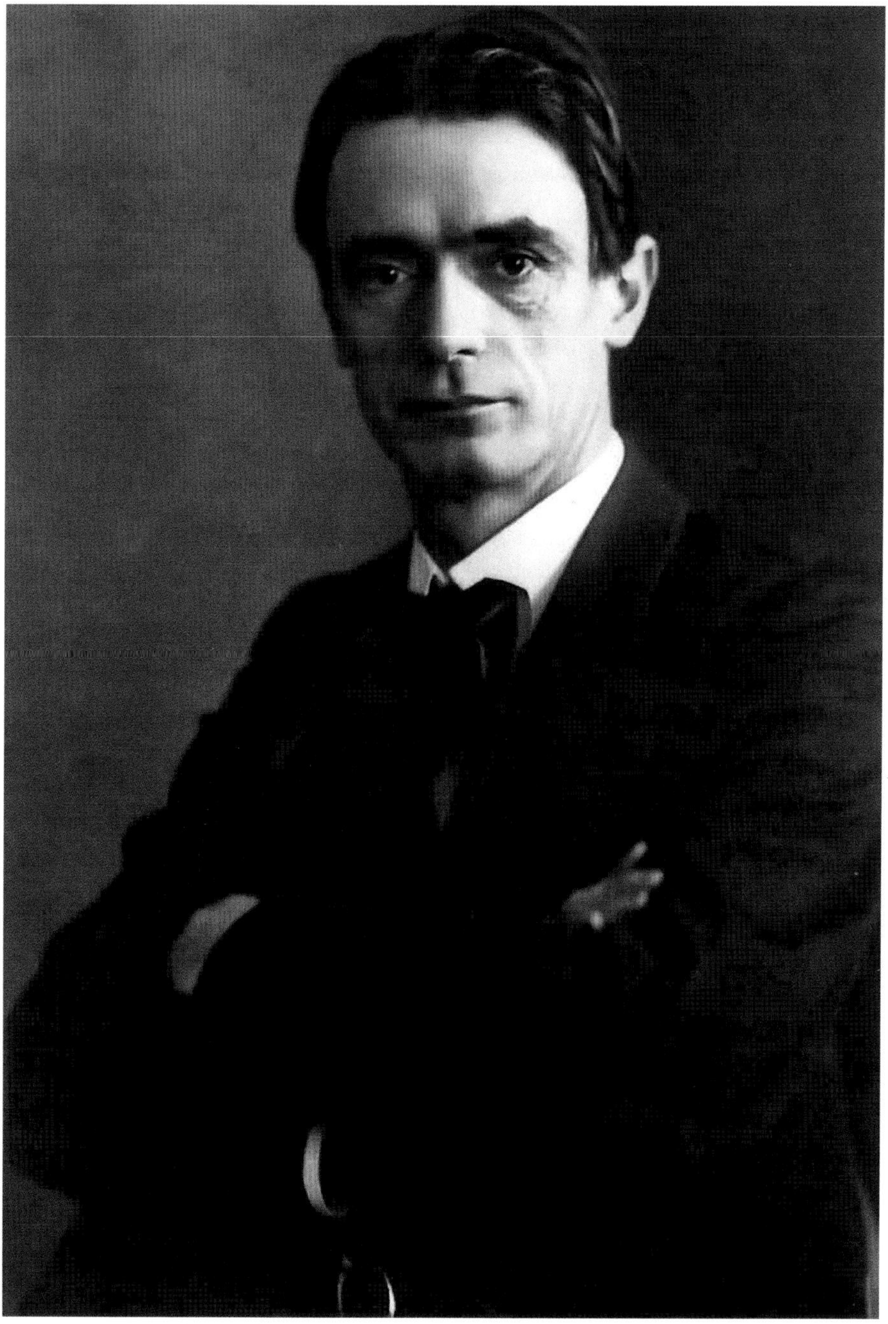

4. *Rudolf Steiner (c. 1905)*

Chapter Three

Aesthetics

1. Of or pertaining to the criticism of taste.
2. Of or pertaining to the sense of the beautiful artistic; concerned with the theory of beauty and the fine arts.

Greek:	*aisthetikos*	—pertaining to sense perception
	aistheta	—perceptible things
	aisthenasthai	—to perceive

3. The branch of philosophy that provides a theory of the beautiful and of the fine arts.
4. The branch of metaphysics concerned with the laws of perception.
5. A doctrine affirming beauty as the basic principle from which all other principles are derived.
6. Philosophy of beauty especially in art.

Aristotle

BEAUTY

Now since the good and the beautiful are different (for the former always implied conduct as its subject, while the beautiful is found also in motionless things), those who assert that the mathematical sciences say nothing of the beautiful or the good are in error. For these sciences say and prove a great deal about them, if they do not expressly mention them, but prove attributes which are their results or their definitions, it is not true to say that they tell us nothing about them. The chief forms of beauty are order and symmetry and definiteness, which the mathematical sciences demonstrate in a special degree. And since these (e.g. order and definiteness) are obviously causes of many things, evidently these sciences must treat this sort of causative principle also (i.e. the beautiful) as in some sense a cause. But we shall speak more plainly elsewhere about these matters.

From *Metaphysics* (1078^a 31–1078^b 6), Book XIII

. . . Beauty varies with the time of life. In a young man beauty is the possession of a body fit to ensure the exertion of running and of contests of strength; which means that he is pleasant to look at; and therefore all-round athletes are the most beautiful, being naturally adapted both for contests of strength and for speed also. For a man in his prime, beauty is fitness for the exertion of warfare, together with a pleasant but at the same time formidable appearance. For an old man, it is to be strong enough for such exertion as is necessary, and to be free from all those deformities of old age which cause pain to others.

From *Rhetoric* (1361^b 2–15), Book I

STANDARD OF ARTISTIC GOODNESS

Every virtue or excellence both brings into good condition the thing of which it is the excellence and makes the work of that thing be done well; e.g. the excellence of the eye makes both the eye and its work good; for it is by the excellence of the eye that we see well.

Similarly the excellence of the horse makes a horse both good in itself and good at running and carrying its rider and at awaiting the attack of the enemy. Therefore, if this is true in every case, the virtue of man also will be the state of character which makes a man good and which makes him do his work well.

1106b . . . we often say of good works of art that it is not possible either to take away or to add anything, implying that excess and defect destroy the goodness of works of art, while the mean preserves it, and good artists, as we say, look to this in their work.

From *Nicomachean Ethics* (1006^{a} 14), Book II

The beautiful is that which is desirable for its own sake, and pleasant, or that, which being good, is pleasurable because it is good.

From *Rhetoric* (1366^{a} 33)

Thomas Aquinas

Thomas Aquinas considered the good and the beautiful as being more or less identical in that goodness is an attribute of beauty, and that the beautiful is also good. He saw however that they differed in their *rationes* (their attributes, intentions or conceptions), and perceived the good as being that which all desire and aspire towards, and the beautiful as that which gives pleasure when perceived or observed (*quod visum placet*).

He distinguished three aspects of the beautiful:

1. *integritas sive perfectio*
2. *debita proportio sive consonantia*
3. *claritas*

We find this in the *Summa Theologica*, 1, 39, 8, where he writes:

> There are three requirements for beauty. Firstly integrity or perfection—for if something is impaired it is ugly. Then there is due proportion or consonance. And also clarity: whence all things that are brightly coloured are called beautiful.

These rather compact definitions can be broadened so that a fuller appreciation of their depth and application within the field of aesthetics can be developed. In order to do this, I have taken the liberty of extending them in two directions: from the linguistic aspect and from the aspect of their conceptual content. In doing so I hope that I have in a sense opened their potential in a creative way.

1. *integritas sive perfectio*

This is usually understood as 'perfect in integrity'. It can also be understood as: having perfection within various conditions—to be perfect in virtuousness, in nobility, in worthiness, or to be perfect in purity, in honourableness and high character. Integrity can also incorporate the idea of wholeness or completeness; that which has indivisibility or one-ness, a universality.

2. *debita proportio sive consonantia*

This is usually interpreted as 'having due proportion', but when extended it encompasses: having harmonious relation; being formed with symmetry; having a perfect relationship of parts within a whole. It can also be

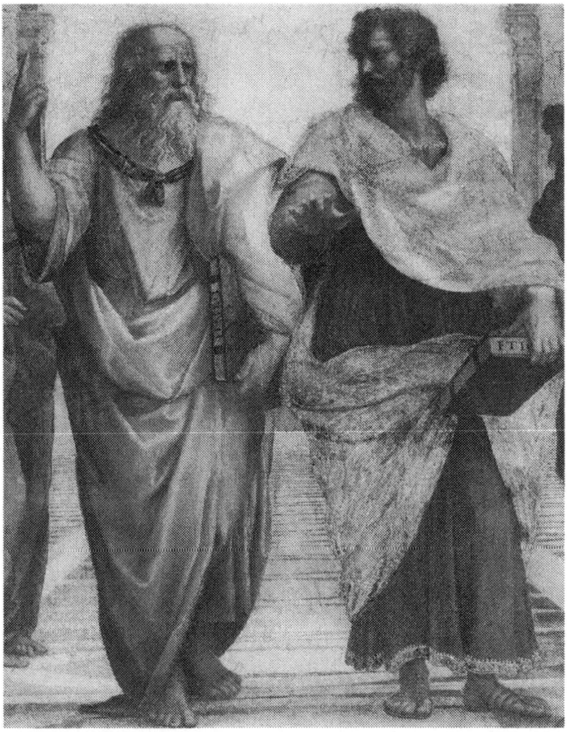

10. Detail from 'The School of Athens' by Raphael, said to be Plato (left) with Aristotle

expressed as: having smooth and flowing joining of details; of having elegant dimensions; of having consonance or classical, symmetrical positioning; or of having balance, consonance and graceful interconnections. In this aspect of the beautiful we can extend Aquinas' definition to include the accepted range of aesthetic attributes which we would usually consider when seeking to understand a work of art or philosophy.

3. *claritas*

Our contemporary term 'clarity' is derived from *claritas*. When extended into the realm of defining the beautiful it can refer to: brilliance; lucidity, luminosity; or being transparent or lucid. '*Claritas*' can also imply: clearness, intelligibility, comprehensibility. We can see that the expression can apply to the realm of philosophical thought, or to the exercise of the mind, in the sense of something being coherent, cognizable, clear-cut and distinct. Within the sense-perceptible world it can be applied to the condition of translucency, clearness and transparency of being.

THE GENERAL NOTION OF GOOD

Summa Theologica 1a.5.4, Article 4: 'What Kind of Causality is Implicit in the Notion of Goodness?'

The Fourth Point:

1. Being good seems to imply not so much being an end or goal as being one of the other kinds of cause. For Dionysius says that *the good is esteemed beautiful.* Now beauty involves the notion of form. Goodness therefore conveys the idea of form.
2. Or another approach; good things pour forth their own being, as Dionysius gives us to understand, saying that *from the good comes all subsistence and existence.* Now pouring out involves the idea of an operative cause. Being good therefore conveys the idea of being an operative cause.
3. Moreover, Augustine says *we exist because God is good.* Now existence comes from God as an operative cause. So being good implies being an operative cause.

On the Other Hand we have the words of Aristotle: *that for the sake of which things exist is their good and their goal.* Being good therefore involves being an end or goal.

Reply: Since good is what all things desire, and this involves the idea of a goal, clearly being good involves being a goal. Nevertheless, presupposed to the idea of good are the notions of operative cause and form.

. . . A good thing is also in fact a beautiful thing, for both epithets have the same basis in reality, namely, the possession of form; and this is why *the good is esteemed beautiful.* Good and beautiful are not however synonymous. For good being *what all things desire* has to do properly with desire and so involves the idea of end (since desire is a kind of movement towards something). Beauty, on the other hand, has to do with knowledge, and we call a thing beautiful when it pleases the eye of the beholder. This is why beauty is a matter of right proportion, for the senses delight in rightly proportioned things as similar to themselves, the sense-faculty being a sort of proportion itself like all other knowing faculties. Now since knowing proceeds by imaging, and images have to do with form, beauty properly involves the notion of form.

Beauty goes with every virtue, nevertheless it excels with temperance, and in two respects. First, because measured and seemly proportion, which Dionysius describes as of the essence of beauty, is the mark of temperateness in general. Next, because the specific virtue of temperance exercises control over the lower levels of human life, namely those of our animal nature, a point to be developed later on. There are forces here of debasement, and because temperance plays such a part in holding them down it is especially credited with beauty.

Summa Theologica, Volume 43, Temperance

In fact there are two kinds of beauty. One is spiritual and it consists in a due ordering and overflowing of spiritual goods (or substance). Everything that proceeds from a lack of spiritual goodness, or that manifests as disorder, is ugly.

Another kind is external beauty which consists as a due ordering of the body.

'*Contra Impugnantes Dei Cultum et Religionem*', 7, ad 9

Aquinas also refers to:

Dionysii de Divinis Nominibus IV, 5–6

All of creation shares in the transcendent beauty of God. All lower beauties are but imperfect manifestations of one highest pulchritudo.

(This is Dionysian mystical aesthetics.)

Rudolf Steiner

The task of art is to take hold of the radiance, the manifestation, of all that which as spirit weaves and lives throughout the world. All genuine art seeks the spirit. Even when art wishes to represent the ugly, the disagreeable, it is concerned not with the sensory-disagreeable as such but with the spiritual which proclaims its nature in the midst of unpleasantness. If the spiritual shines through the ugly, even the ugly becomes beautiful. In art, it is upon a relation to the spiritual that beauty depends.

In the German language, we speak of the beautiful as '*das Schæne*' (*Schöne*) which is related to 'shining', and the ugly as '*das Hæssliche*' (*Hässliche*) which is related to 'hateful'. The beautiful shines; it brings its inner nature to the surface. It is the distinguishing nature of the beautiful not to hide itself, but to carry its essence into outer configuration. Thus beauty reveals inwardness through outer form, and radiates into the world. If we were to speak in this sense of beauty's opposite, we could call it the concealed or non-radiant—that which holds back its being, refusing to reveal itself outwardly. To put it another way, 'the beautiful' can designate something objective. If we treat its opposite just as objectively we would have to speak of concealment, of something whose outer aspect belies what it really is. But here subjectivity enters, for we cannot love what conceals itself, showing a false countenance; we dislike it, or even hate it. In this way, the ugly evokes quite a different emotional response than the beautiful; we do not respond to it out of the same depths of our nature.

The fact that the German word for 'beautiful' (*Schöne*) bears a relationship to 'shine' suggests that the beautiful has a relationship to the spiritual outside of us, rather than remaining within our personal emotions. The ugly, in this sense, cannot radiate outwardly and remains within our dislike or antipathy. What we see in the physical world, exists. It does not necessarily need to shine. It is the spiritual that shines, radiating into the sense-perceptible and proclaiming its being, its presence and activity in the sense-world. By speaking objectively of the beautiful in this way we can understand the beautiful as having a spiritual element or aspect which is revealing itself in the world through art.

The Arts and their Mission, Dornach, 9 June 1923

Throughout all ages of conscious human evolution, truth, beauty and goodness have been regarded as the three great ideals of mankind. It may be said that these three ideals, truth, beauty and goodness are looked upon instinctively as the great goals which give human striving its character.

When someone considers the truth concerning a fact, he finds himself in harmony with the feeling he has of his physical body and even of the connection his physical body has with his pre-earthly life... Nothing strengthens man's primary and true feeling of existence as does a sense of truth and truthfulness... This feeling of existence is connected with the fact that we experience the spirit within the physical body. So we must recognize the close correlation between our physical body and the ideal of truth.

The feeling we have of our existence within our etheric body is made stronger by the experience of beauty... If we develop a right feeling for beauty, this means that we dwell rightly in the etheric body, the body of formative forces... To have a sense of beauty is to recognize the etheric body.

In the face of beauty the ancient Greek sensed that he was filled with an inner depth of feeling, that he was inwardly warmed and illumined. One might almost say that he felt himself inwardly endowed with divinity. This was the experience of feeling in the etheric body... The ancient Greek felt cold all over when he met ugliness and if the ugliness was very intense it even made his flesh creep. This real experience of the etheric body was still keenly felt in earlier times.

A wholly industrial city is a delightful abode for all those demons whose desire it is to make man forget his pre-earthly existence in the spiritual world. For earthly life itself, a link is created with the world of the spirit when a human being is warmed with a feeling for beauty. In all education, in all outward manifestations of culture and civilization, we should never underestimate the significance of beauty. The philistine who disregards beauty wants to create on earth an abode into which the sun of the spirit does not shine, and where he can walk about as it were in spiritual obscurity.

For a person to be truthful means that they have a right connection with their spiritual past. For a person to have a sense for beauty means that they do not deny their connections with the spirit in the present. For a person to be good means that they nurture a seed for a spiritual world in the future... When a person lives in a true spirit of goodness their deeds on earth engender forces which endure beyond the gate of death . . . true and genuine goodness, for a good deed inspired by love leads us to an experience of the astral body . . . The purpose of these three ideals, of truth, beauty and goodness is to give expression to the way in which a person can recognize his full human potential.

'Truth, Beauty and Goodness', from *Art in the Light of Mystery Wisdom*, Dornach, 19 January 1923

Chapter Four

Colour

1. The appearance of objects or light sources described in terms of the individuals' perception of them, involving hue, lightness and saturation for objects, and hue, brightness and saturation for light sources.
2. The characteristics of light by which the individual is made aware of objects or light sources through the receptors of the eye, described in terms of dominant, wavelength, luminance and purity.
3. Sensation produced on the eye by rays of light when resolved, as by a prism, into different wavelengths.
4. One, or any mixture, of the constituents into which light can be separated as in a spectrum or rainbow.

Aristotle

I. Colours are simple which belong to the elements, fire, air, water and earth. For air and water are naturally white in themselves, while fire and the sun are golden. The earth is also naturally white, but seems coloured because it is dyed. This becomes clear when we consider ashes; for they become white when the moisture which caused their dyeing is burned out of them; but not completely so, for they are also dyed by smoke, which is black. In the same way sand becomes golden, because the fiery red and black tints the water. The colour black belongs to the element of things while they are undergoing a transformation of their nature. But the other colours are evidently due to mixture, when they are blended with each other. For darkness follows when light fails.

But black appears to us in three ways. In the first, that which is not seen is, generally speaking, black naturally (for any light from such things is reflected as black); or secondly, black is that from which no light is conveyed to the eyes; for that which is not seen, when the surrounding region is seen, gives an impression of black. Thirdly, all things appear black of the kind from which a very small amount of light is reflected. This is why shadows appear to be black.

In the same way water appears to be black when it is rough, as for instance the ripple of the sea; for owing to the roughness of the surface few rays can fall on it, and the light is scattered, and so what is in shadow appears to be black. It is for the same reason that cloud appears to be black when it is very thick. It is just the same with water and air when the light does not entirely penetrate them. For these also appear to be black when deep, for very few rays of light are totally reflected; for all those parts which are in between the light parts seem to be black because of the darkness. One can learn from many facts that darkness is not a colour at all, but is merely an absence of light, and particularly from the fact that it is not possible to perceive in darkness the character or shape of anything, as it is in the case of visible objects.

But that light is the colour of fire is clear from the fact that it is discovered to have no colour but this, and because it alone is visible by itself, whereas all other things are visible by means of it. This point must be further considered. For some things which are neither fire nor forms of fire seem to produce light by nature. Unless the colour of fire is light, light is not the colour of fire alone; but it is possible that this colour does not belong to fire merely, but that light is actually its colour. Certainly visibility is impossible in any way except by light, just as the visibility of all other bodies is only possible by the appearance of colour. But the colour black is seen when air and water are burned by fire; thus all things grow black when burning, such as wood and coals when the fire is quenched, and the smoke from potter's clay when the moisture which is in the clay separates and is burned. For this reason smoke that arises from fat and oily matter is the blackest, such as from oil, pitch and a pinewood torch, because these burn to the greatest extent and have continuity of substance. Those things also become black through which water flows, when the moisture of those which are grown over with moss first dries up, like the plaster in walls. Stones behave in the same way in the presence of water. For these too when moss-grown and afterwards dried become black in colour.

These then are all the simple colours.

II. The other colours derived from these by mixture in greater or smaller proportions make many different varieties. By greater and small proportions I mean such as red and purple, by mixture such as white and black, which when mixed gives an appearance of grey. So when what is black and shady is mixed with light the result is red. For we see that, when what is black is mixed with the light of the sun and fire, the result is always red, and black things when burned always change to the colour red; for smoky flame and coal, when it is burned through, are seen to have a red colour. Purple is gay and bright whenever the rays of the sun are a weak mixture of white and shady. Consequently at the hours of sunrise and sunset the air seems to have a purple tint, the sun being at its rising or setting. For its rays being weak at the time are cast upon the air when it is inclined to be dark. The sea again has a purple tinge when the waves rise at an angle, and consequently are in shadow; for the sun's rays striking feebly at an angle cause the colour to appear purple. The same thing is seen to occur with plumage; for when exposed to the light it has a purple tint. When less light strikes it, it is of that dark tint which men call grey-brown; when, however, the light is strong and mixed with primary black it becomes red. But when it is light and shining as well it changes to flame colour.

As far as mixture with each other is concerned we must begin our inquiry by making a mixture starting with an observed base, but not assuming a similar origin for all. For some colours are not simple, but the same relation applies to some of the compound colours as the simple ones bear to them, because in a sense the simple colours must be mixed with one of these compounds, and we must not assume it to be equally obvious in every case even on a close inspection. For when we speak of a mixture of purple and red, we must explain on similar lines those which are a mixture of these two and produce another colour, but must not expect a similar appearance. We must then base our assumptions and our examination of mixtures on what has been prepared before, for instance that the colour of dark wine occurs when sunlight rays are mixed with what is pure black and what is glittering, like the berries of the grape; for their colour is said to be wine-dark at the moment of ripening; for, when they are growing black, red changes to purple. According to the method we have laid down we must inquire into all the variations of colour, finding similarity of colour in objects undergoing movement according to their actual appearance, finding similar explanations of the mixing in each case, even in the case of those which both by origin and through mixture produce the appearance, and by bringing forward convincing proof. But we must make our investigation into these things not by mixing these colours as painters do, but by comparing the rays which are reflected from those to which we have already referred. For one could especially consider the mixing of rays in nature. But we require convincing proof and a consideration of similarities, if the origin of the colours is to become obvious. This is especially the case with the light of the sun, and that which comes from fire, air and water; for these being mixed in greater or less proportions produce in a sense all the colours. One must also base conclusions on the similarities of the other colours, when mixed with the rays of the sun; for coal, smoke, rust and sulphur and plumage when mixed, some with the rays of the sun and some with fire, provide many variations of colour. Other colours, again, must be considered in ripening, occurring as they do in plants and fruit, hair and feathers and all such things.

III. We must not, however, neglect the variegated and the ill-defined among colours, and the quantities to which their occurrence is due. We shall find that it is because they have an unequal and disproportionate share of light and shade; for the difference between light and shade is a quantitative difference of more and less, so that by themselves and when mixed with colours they cause change of

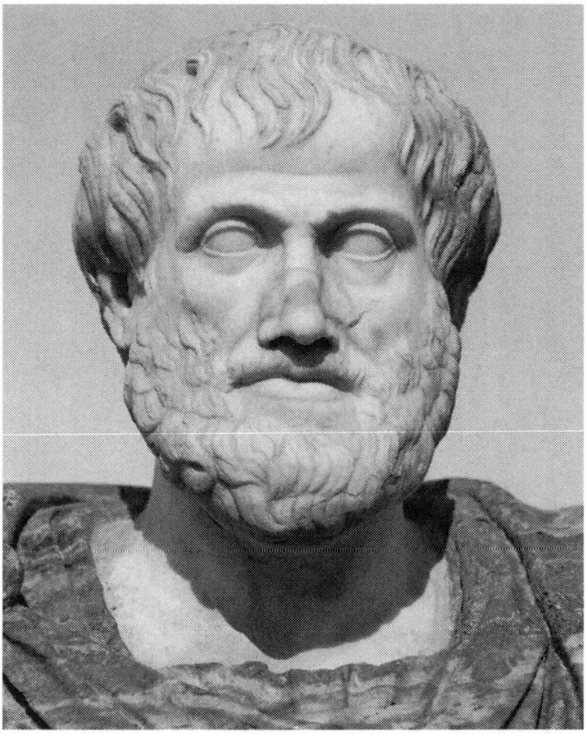

11. Aristotle, Roman copy of a Greek bronze bust by Lysippos

colour, either because the colours mixed differ in quantity and strength, or because they have not the same proportions. For purple exhibits a large number of variations, and so does red and white, and each of the other colours, both in the matter of greater and less, and in their mixture with each other and in their purity. It also makes a difference whether the colour mixed is bright and shining, or on the contrary dark and dull. Shining is nothing but the continuity and intensity of light. A golden colour appears when what is yellow and sunny gleams with great intensity. This is why the necks of doves and drops of water appear golden when light is reflected from them. Some objects, when smoothed by rubbing or by other forces, exhibit varied and different colours, like silver when it is rubbed and gold, bronze and steel. Some kinds of stones show different colours, for though black they draw white lines, because they are originally composed of small elements which are thick and black, and by the dyeing process which takes place when they are made, all the passages through which the dyeing passes are coloured, so that a different appearance is given to the colour. But what is rubbed off from them is no longer golden in appearance, nor bronze, nor has it any other such tinge, but is entirely black, because by the rubbing the passages through which the dyeing takes place are broken up, but originally they are of the same colour. For when the former colour is no longer obvious to us, because the dyeing process is dissipated, we see the colour which naturally belongs to them; and so they all appear black. But in the process of rubbing each of them to a homogeneous and smooth surface, as in treading on a touchstone, they lose their blackness, and recover their colour, the dye showing through when there is contact and continuity. But in the case of things burned and being disintegrated and melting in the fire those exhibit most colours where the smoke is light and misty and the colours are dark, like the smoke that arises from sulphur and from rusty bronze, and all substances which are dense and smooth such as silver. But other cases of variety are those which have dark colours and some measure of smoothness, such as water, clouds and birds' plumage. For these owing to their smoothness and the rays that fall upon them, mixed in various ways, produce various colours, just as darkness does.

We do not see any of the colours pure as they really are, but all are mixed with others; or if not mixed with any other colour they are mixed with rays of light and with shadows, and so they appear different and not as they are. Consequently things appear different according to whether they are seen in shadow or in sunlight, in a hard or a soft light, and according to the angle at which they are seen and in accordance with other differences as well. Those which are seen in the light of the fire or the moon and by the rays of a lamp differ by reason of the light in each case: and also by the mixture of the colours with each other; for in passing through each other they are coloured; for when light falls on something, and, being tinted by it, becomes reddish or greenish, and then the reflected light falls on another colour, being again mixed by it, it takes on still another mixture of colour. And by being affected in this way, continually but imperceptibly, it sometimes reaches the eyes as a mixture of many colours, but producing the sensation of the most predominant; so in water things appear more watery and things seen in mirrors appear to have similar colours to those in the mirrors. This also happens, one would suppose, in the case of air. So that all colours are a mixture of three things, the light, the medium through which the light is seen, such as water and air, and thirdly, the colours forming the ground, from which the light happens to be reflected. But the white and the transparent, when it is very thin, appears misty in colour. But over what is dense a haze invariably appears, as in the case of water, glass and air, when it is dense. For, as the rays from all directions fail owing to the density, we cannot see accurately into their inner parts. But the air when examined from near-by seems to have no colour (for owing to its thinness it is controlled by the rays and is divided up by them, because they are denser and show right through it), but when examined in depth, the air appears from very near-by to be blue in colour because of its rarity. For where the light fails, there, being penetrated by darkness at this point, it appears blue. But, when dense, just as with water, it is the whitest of all things.

IV. All dyed things take their colour from what dyes them. For many are coloured by the flowers of plants, many by the roots, many again by bark or wood or leaves or fruit. Many again are coloured by earth, by foam, and many by ink; others again are coloured by animal juices, such as purple by the murex. Others again by wine, by smoke, by dust, or by sea, as is the case with the hair among sea creatures; for these are all made reddish by the sea. This is true, speaking generally, of all those which have distinctive colours. For when the colours enter the passages of that which is being dyed together with moisture and heat, when they are dried they take their colours from them. And so it is often washed out of them, when the dye flows out of the passages. But the steeping in alum in the dyeing process produces many differences and mixtures, and so do the qualities of the substances dyed, as has been said before in the case of mixtures. When black fleeces are dyed they do not become all equally bright in colour, because their passages are dyed when the dye enters into them, but the spaces in between the hair receive no dye. These being white and lying side by side with the colours makes the dye appear brighter; the black parts on the other hand are shadowy and dark. Consequently what is called brown-grey is brighter when on black wool than on white. For in this case the dye appears purer, being mingled with the rays of the black. By itself the space in between the passages is not noticed because of its smallness, just as tin is not noticed when it is mixed with bronze, nor any other such thing. The colours of things dyed vary in kind according to the reasons we have outlined.

V. Hair and plumage and flowers and fruit and all plants can in many ways be seen to take on changes of colours at the time of ripening; but now we have to consider what are the primary sources of the colours which belong naturally to each species, what changes they exhibit and from what and for what reason they are thus affected, and whether any other difficulties follow these facts. The inquiry depends on the following facts. The primary colour of all plants is green; for shoots and leaves and fruit are all green to begin with. One can see exactly the same thing in rain water; when the water has stood for a long time, as it dries up again it becomes green in colour. This happens logically, and in all growing things this is the first colour that obtains. For all water that stands for a long time is green originally, being mixed with the rays of the sun, but it gradually grows black, but becomes green again when mixed with fresh water. For anything moist, as has been said, as it grows old by itself and dries up, becomes black, as plaster does in its receptacles; for all things which are always in water become black, because the moisture does not grow cold and dry, but all that is drained out and exposed to the sun becomes green because the yellow is mixed with the black. Or rather as the moist part blackens, the green becomes very dark and of the colour of a leek. Consequently the older shoots are much blacker than the young ones; the latter are yellower because the moisture in them has not yet turned black. For as their growth becomes slower and their moisture lasts for a long time, as the moisture becomes very black as it cools, it changes to leek-green by being mixed with pure black.

But in the case of those in which the moisture is not mixed with the rays of the sun, their white colour persists, unless it grows black by lasting a long time and drying up first. Consequently, in all plants the parts above the earth are green at first, but beneath the earth stalks and roots are white.* Shoots, again, if they are below the earth are white, but if the earth is removed from around them they all become green right from the first, as has been said before, because the moisture which passes down into them through the shoots has this colour naturally and in the case of fruits this is soon spent on growth; but when they no longer grow, it is because the heat cannot control the food which flows into them, but on the contrary the moisture is exhausted by the heat. Then all the fruits become ripe; and as the moisture in them is also warmed by the sun and the heat of the atmosphere, each combines to take the colours from the juices, just as those which are dyed from the flowers. So they are coloured

* Aristotle does not understand photosynthesis, but he does know that the green is due to the sun's action.

little by little, and most of all those which are turned towards the sun and the warmth.

So that the colours change in accordance with the seasons. This is obvious; those of a green hue all change as they grow ripe in their natural colour. For they are white, black, grey, yellow, blackish, dark, dull-coloured red, wine-dark and saffron and exhibit almost all the differences of colour. But since the largest number of colours appear when more are mixed with each other, it is obvious that the colours in plants must have the same mixture; for the moisture penetrating through them, and washing all colours through with it, produces all the possible colours. And as this is warmed up in the ripening of the fruit by the sun and the warmth of the air, each of the colours becomes fixed by itself, some more quickly and some more slowly, as occurs in dyeing by the murex. For when they have cut this open and drained from it all the moisture, and have poured this out and boiled it in vessels, at first none of the colours is quite obvious in the dye, because as the liquid boils more, and the colours which are still in it get more mixed, each of them exhibits many and varied differences; for there is black and white, and dull, and misty, and finally all becomes purple when the boiling is complete, so that in the mixture none of the other colours is visible by itself.

The same thing occurs with fruits. For in many of them owing to the fact that the ripening of all the colours does not take place at once, but some form earlier and others later, they change from one to the other, as in grapes and dates. For some of these become red at first, but as the black is formed in them they turn to wine-dark; but at last they become purplish, when the red colour is mixed with a large quantity of pure black. For those colours which are formed later, when they prevail, cause the previous colours to change.

This is most obvious in the case of the black fruits; for the larger number of them, as has been said, changing from their initial green redden and become tawny, but they soon change again from the red and become purple owing to the unmixed black which exists in them. But this proves the point; for cuttings, and shoots, and leaves of all such plants are red, because this kind of colour exists in them, since it is obvious that the black fruits share in both these colours; for the juice of all such plants is wine-dark.

But in their order of origin the red comes before the black. This is obvious; for the ground upon which the drops fall and speaking generally any spot at which there is a moderate fall of water in dark places all change first from a greenish colour to red, and the ground becomes as though blood has been recently spilled on the spot in which the green takes on the ripening; at the end this becomes very black and blueish. The same thing happens with fruits. In their case it is easy to see that the colour of the fruit changes, as the colours are laid on it afterwards. For the fruit of the pomegranate and the petals of the rose are white to begin with, but at last as the juices in them get tinted by ripening, they become shaded off and change again to the colour of sea-purple and red. Other things have more colours in them, such as the juice of the poppy and the skins of the olive for the latter is white at first, just like the fruit of the pomegranate, but after having grown white again it changes to the colour red, and at last by being mixed with black it becomes blueish. Consequently the leaves of the poppy are reddish on top, because their ripening comes quickly, but their other parts are black at the bottom, as this colour prevails in them, as is also the case with the fruit; for at last it becomes black. In the case of those plants which have one colour only, such as white, black, red or purple, the fruits of all these persist in having the same type of colour, when once they change from green to another colour. The flowers are in some cases of the same colour as the fruit, as is true of the pomegranate; for both its fruit and its flower become reddish; in some cases there is a great difference in colour, for instances in the bay and the ivy; for the flower of all these species is yellow, but the fruit of the latter is black and of the former red. The same thing is true of the apple-tree; for its flower is white tending to grow purple, while its fruit is golden. The flower of the poppy is red, and its fruit partly black and partly white, according to the ripening of the juices in it at different times. One can see this in many cases; for some fruits, as has already been said, exhibit many variations at the time of ripening.

So it happens that very different scents and juices are associated with both flower and fruit. This is still more obvious in the case of the flowers themselves, for, in the same petal, part may be black and part red and in some cases part may be white and part purplish. This is specially true of the iris;* for this plant has many differences in colour during its ripening, as is also the case with grapes, when they come to ripen. So in their case the tips of the flowers ripen, but these at the extremities have much less colour than the rest. In some of them the moisture is, so to speak, burned out of them before they take on their own proper ripening. So the flowers remain of one

* The purple iris with a yellow centre is common in Greece.

colour, but the fruit changes as it ripens. Some plants owing to the smallness of their food ripen quickly, but the fruits owing to their quantity of moisture change at the time of their ripening into all their natural colours. This is clear, as has been said before, especially in the case of dyeing with colour. For sometimes to begin with, when they are dyeing purple and put in the blood-red dye, it becomes grey-brown, black and sky-blue; but when the dye is boiled enough, it becomes quite purple, gay, and bright.

In the same way many of the flowers must differ from the colours of the fruits, some receiving an excess and some a deficiency of their natural colours, owing to the fact that in some the ripening is incomplete, and in some complete. For these reasons it happens that flowers and fruit differ from each other in colour; but the leaves of most trees become yellow at the end, because, when their food fails, they dry before they change into their natural colours; in the same way when fruits fall off some become yellow in colour because their food has failed them before the time of ripening. This is also true of corn and of all growing things; for they all become yellow at the end. For the moisture in them being no longer blackened by drying causes the change of colour. For when growing black and mixed with green it becomes, as has been said, greenish; but as the black grows steadily weaker, the colour changes back again gradually to green, and at last becomes yellow. So the leaves of the parsley, purslane and of some other plants grow red as they ripen. Except for those which grow dry quickly, these become yellow because their food fails before they ripen. The differences in the colours of plants are most reasonably accounted for by the reasons we have given.

VI. Hair, plumage, skin of horses, cattle, sheep, men and all other living creatures are white and grey and red and black for the same reason; white when the moisture which possesses its own natural colour dries up, and black on the other hand when the moisture about the skin at birth, as happens in all other cases, grows black when it grow old and has lasted a long time because of its quantity; for the complexion and the skin of all such is black. Those are grey, red, yellow and other colours, which dry before the moisture in them changes completely to black. Those in whom this change takes place unevenly have all kinds of variegated colours. So everything accords with the skin in colour, since men of ruddy complexion have pale red hair, and dark-skinned men have black hair. But if in any part of the body white leprosy has broken out, all have also white hairs in this place, as in the beasts of varied colours.

So also the hair and plumage is in accordance with the skin, and what applies to the parts applies also to the whole body. The same is true of the hoofs, talons, bills and horns; for in the black animals they are black and in the white white, because in all these cases the food passes to the outer envelope through the skin. It can be seen from many facts that this is the reason. For the heads of all infants at birth are red because of their small amount of food. But this is obvious; for the hair grows weak and thin and short at first on all infants. But as their age increases the hair grows black, as they themselves get coloured by the amount of food that flows in. Similarly when the hair of the body grows and the beard at the time of adolescence, the hairs are reddish to begin with, as the moisture dries quickly because there is but little of it, but as more food travels to the part the hair grows black. But the hairs on the body remain red for the longest time owing to lack of nourishment, since as long as it grows these also continue to grow black, as on other parts of the body and on the head. But this is clear; for in all living creatures which have long hair, speaking generally those near the body are blacker, while those at the extremities are more golden. The hair of sheep, horses and men are so, because the least amount of food is conveyed to those parts, and so they dry quickly. But even the plumage of black birds is blackest near the body and lighter at the extremities. The same thing is true of the parts about the neck, and speaking generally those which receive but little nourishment. This is clear; for before the period of becoming grey all the hair changes colour and becomes red, because the failing food supply dries quickly. But at last it is white, before the moisture grows black, as the food in those parts is matured. This is most evident in beasts of burden; for the hair of all such grows white. For as these parts are unable to draw their sustenance because of the feebleness of the heat, the moisture dries quickly and becomes white. So with men the hair about the temples most readily grows grey, and generally speaking about the parts that are weak and hard worked.

Most of all does the change to this colour take place when it changes its own nature. For a hare has been born white, and has also been seen black; so has a stag and a bear, and similarly a quail, a partridge and a swallow. For when they are weak at birth, all such things are white owing to the shortage of sustenance, because they ripen before their time. So, too, in the case of children; at first they have white heads and eyelids and eyebrows, as is true in each case when they approach old age. Obviously this affection is due to weakness and shortage of sustenance. Consequently most of the white animals are weaker than the black; for before their growth is complete, they are white while developing owing to shortage of sustenance, just as is true of fruits which happen to be diseased; for these ripen much more quickly owing to their weakness. But some creatures are born white and are very superior to the rest, as for instance horses and dogs. These change from their natural colour to white because they are well nourished. For the moisture in them not lasting a long time but being expended on their growth does not become black. Most of these are moist and fleshy because they are well nourished. So that not even the white of the hair changes. This is obvious; for the black parts become reddish before they go grey because their sustenance is failing and becoming riper, but white is the last stage.

Yet there are some who suppose that all things become black because the food is burned up by the heat, just like the blood and other things, but they are wrong. For some living creatures are black to start with, such as dogs, goats and cattle, and speaking generally those whose skins and hair have sustenance from the beginning, but are less so as their age advances. And yet on this assumption it ought not to be so, but the hair of all such creatures should grow blacker at their prime, at which time the heat in them is strongest, and they should be more white at the beginning. For in every case the heat is much more feeble at the beginning than at the time at which the hair is beginning to grow white. This is clear in the case of those which are white. For some have the whitest skin from the start, those namely which have the greatest sustenance at the beginning, and in which the moisture does not dry before its time. But as their age advances they become yellow, because later on less food passes into them. But others are yellow to begin with, and whitest at their prime, just as among birds the colours change when the food in them fails. And this is the proof; for they all grow yellow round the neck, and speaking generally in those parts which go short when the food begins to fail. And this is clear; for as red changes into black and black again into red, so does white change to yellow. This happens in the case of plants; for some revert from the latter state of ripeness back to the former. This is most obvious in the case of the pomegranate. For the kernels are red to start with, and so are the leaves through scarcity of digested food, but later on they change back again into a greenish colour, when much food flows into them and the ripening cannot exercise the same degree of control; but at last, as the food is assimilated, the colour becomes red again.

Speaking generally we may say of the hair and plumage, that they all admit changes, in some cases as we have said because food fails, in others on the other hand because it is in excess. Consequently some hairs at some period of its growth and some at others are whitest and blackest, since the plumage even of ravens changes to a yellow tinge at last, when the food in them fails. But in the case of hair none ever changes in such a way as to have red, purple or green nor any other such colour, because all such colours occur when the rays of the sun are mixed with them, but in the case of hair, which is moist all change takes place within the flesh, and it does not involve any mixture. This is obvious; for initially plumage is not at all like this in colour, but all the varied plumage of birds is, so to speak, black, such as the peacock, the pigeon and the swallow; but later on the plumage takes on all these varied hues, when the ripening of the body has taken place, both in the feather and in the crests, so that in these cases as with plants the ripening of the colours takes place outside the body. So the remainder of living creatures, both water animals and reptiles and shell-fish, have all sorts of colours, as the ripening in them is considerable. From what we have said one could best conduct an investigation into the question of colours.

From: Aristotle, *Minor Works*, Vol. 14, 'On Colour' or '*De Coloribus*'. Transl. W. S. Hett (Loeb Classical Library, Cambridge, Mass., 1980). Further references to Aristotle's discourses on colour are found in his '*De anima*' in *Libri Meteorologicorum* and in *De sensu et sensato*.

Note: The author of this work is aware that the source of the treatise 'On Colour' or '*De Coloribus*' is questioned, and that in some instances it is attributed to a later follower of the Peripatetic School, rather than to Aristotle himself. It is included in this overview on colour due to its contents and approach, being so intimately related to the thought and methodology of Aristotle, and to the ensuing work on colour, furthered by Rudolf Steiner.

Thomas Aquinas

Human Intelligence

But seeing does not take place by abstracting images from colours, but by colours being impressed on the sight. Neither, therefore, does understanding happen by way of something being abstracted from sense images, but by an impression made on the intellect by sense images.

Summa Theologica, 1a, 85, 1 (Volume 12)

From Thomas' Teaching concerning the Heart

From the heart every movement of the body, and therefore also speech, the formation of the '*verbum oris*', the mouth's word, orginates. The rhythm of the pulse-beat follows the laws of the heavenly movements: but disturbances of the rhythm come from passions that arise in the earthly body.

In the heart given to God passions are purified into virtues: as for instance, the burning red of anger becomes the luminant red of charity.

Rudolf Steiner on Thomas Aquinas (Chapter V, 'The Application of Intelligence to the Human Body')

'Whether Sorrow is more Harmful to the Body than other Passions of the Soul?' It would seem that sorrow is not most harmful to the body.

Obj. I: For sorrow has a spiritual being in the Soul. But those things which have only a spiritual being do not cause change in the body, as is evident with regard to the intentions of colours, the images of which are in the air and do not give colour to bodies. Therefore sorrow is not harmful to the body.

Summa Theologica 1, 2 (Question 37, Article 4)

'How the Intellectual Soul Knows Itself and All Within Itself. Whether the Intellectual Soul Knows Itself by Its Essence?'

. . . Everything is knowable so far as it is in act, and not according as it is in its potency, for a thing is a being, and is true, and therefore knowable, according as it is actual. This is quite clear as regards sensible things for the eye does not see what is potentially coloured, but what is actually coloured . . .

. . . the intellect knows itself not by its essence, but by its act.

(Question 87. Article 1)

LIGHT AND COLOUR

Summa Theologica, 1a. 67, 3 (Volume 10, 'The Work of Differentiation'), Article 3, 'Is Light a Quality?'

The Third Point:

1. It seems that light is not a quality. For every quality remains in a subject even after its active cause is removed, as heat remains in water after it is taken from the fire. But light does not remain in air when the light source is taken away. Therefore, light is not a quality.
2. Moreover, every physical quality has a contrary, as cold is the opposite of hot, and black of white. But there is no contrary to light, darkness being merely the absence of light. Therefore, light is not a physical quality.
3. Moreover, any cause is superior to its effect. But light from heavenly bodies causes substantial forms in those below. It also gives a spiritual existence to colours, since it renders them actually visible. Therefore, light is not merely a physical quality but rather a substantial form, or something spiritual.

On the Other Hand, John Damascene holds that light is a kind of quality.

Reply: Some have maintained that light does not have a natural presence in air, the way colour is in the wall, but rather an intentional presence, like an image of colour in air.

But this cannot be the case, for two reasons. First, because light is a predicate of air, air becoming actually luminous. Colour, however, is not such a predicate, since air is not said to be 'coloured'. Secondly, because light produces a physical effect, in that bodies become warm through the rays on the sun. But intentional beings do not cause physical changes.

Again, others maintain that light is the substantial form of the sun. But this also looks to be impossible, for two reasons. First, because

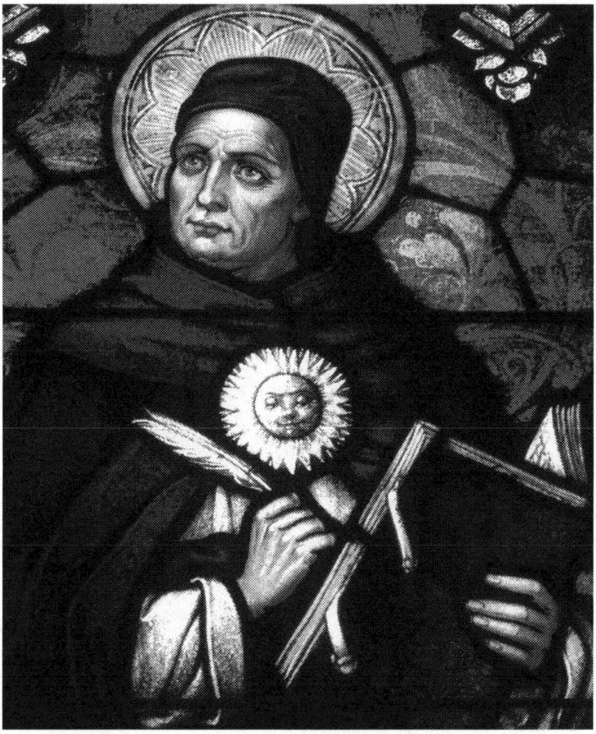

12. Thomas Aquinas, stained glass window from St Joseph's Catholic Church (Kentucky)

no substantial form is directly perceptible to sense, for the essentials in a thing are grasped by intelligence, as Aristotle holds; yet light is directly visible. Secondly, because it is impossible that what is a substantial form in one thing be an accidental form in another. A substantial form is what makes a thing to be of a certain type, and therefore it is always found in everything of that type. Light, however, is not the substantial form of air, for if it were, air would cease to exist when not illuminated. Consequently, it cannot be the substantial form of the sun.

The truth, then, is that just as heat is an active quality deriving from the substantial form of fire, so light is an active quality deriving from the substantial form of the sun, or of any other body that is self-illuminating should any such exist. An indication that some may in fact exist is that rays from different stars produce different effects in bodies of various types.*

*St Thomas acknowledged and gave limited credence to the teachings of medieval astrologers.

Summa Theologica (Volume 21, 'Fear and Anger', Question 46, 'The Nature of Anger'), Inquiry no. 1: 'Is Anger a Specific Emotion?'

Reply no 3: Anger has no contrary distinct from it because within anger itself there is no contrariety. Thus anger is produced by contrary emotions—by hope, whose object is agreeable, and by sadness, whose object is disagreeable. There is something like this in intermediate colours, in which the only contrariety is that of the pure colours, of which they are composed.

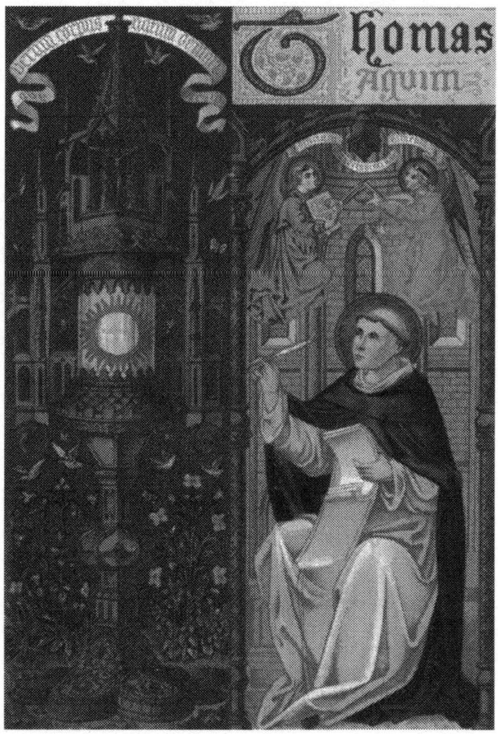

Rudolf Steiner

COLOUR IN MINERALS

The heavenly bodies (i.e. the planets) which surround the earth and belong to its planetary system were once connected with the whole Earth; they were separated in just the same way as the moon. This exodus of the planets is connected with the intrinsic colouring of lifeless things. Solids have become coloured, could become coloured, because the Earth was freed from those forces which were within it when it was united with the planets. These forces could then work upon the Earth from outside, evoking the inner power of the cosmos in the colours of minerals. This is, in fact, what the minerals received, from what has left the Earth and now acts from the cosmos. We see that the mystery is much more deeply hidden than with the green of the plant. But just because it is hidden we are able to penetrate more deeply into its nature, not only into the life of the plants but right into the lifeless minerals. So in our consideration of the colouring of solid matter, we come to something not taken into account at all by present-day physics. We are led to cosmic effects. We cannot understand the colouring of lifeless objects at all if we do not know its connection with what the Earth has retained as inner forces through the departure of the other planets from it.

We will have to explain how one mineral or another may be red, for instance, because of the interaction of the Earth and one of the planets, say Mars or Mercury; or how some may be a yellow colour because of the interaction of the Earth and Jupiter or Venus, and so on. The colours of minerals will always be a riddle so long as the connection between the Earth and what lies outside it in the cosmos is not understood . . .

. . . But if we wish to understand what shines out from the inner nature of material objects and how the once fluctuating colours of the spectrum have now become set within solid bodies, (or forms), we must remind ourselves that what is out in the cosmos today was once within the earth, and is the origin of everything on earth which has a fluctuating quality, even if this is to some extent weighed down. We must look outside the earth for the cause of what lies hidden under the minerals' surface; that is the essential thing.

'Colour in Matter—Painting out of Colour', Dornach, 8 May 1921

The human eye and all its veins and nerve strands is constructed with the imagination of spiritual beings—it is the outcome of live imagination.

So when you look at a green jewel, just because your eye is an organ which is full of imagination, you cannot see it in any other way than as it was constructed out of the green colour of the world of spirit infinite years ago. The moment you see the green jewel you transport your eye back into far distant ages and the green appears to you because divine spiritual beings created this substance out of the spiritual world, out of the green colour belonging to the spirit. The moment you see green, red, blue or yellow in precious stones you look back into the infinitely far-distant past.

If a topaz is put in front of us we cannot see it merely in this moment, we have to see a time perspective. And as the jewel takes us back in time we look at the first beginnings of Earth creation, and because we see it being created out of the spirit, we see it coloured.

. . . It is really that the divine spiritual beings who created stones long ages ago come alive in the colours and stimulate a living memory in us of their past creations. When we see lifeless nature coloured, it is that our mutual relation with lifeless nature (i.e. the mineral), is making a memory of the far distant past become a reality.

By looking at jewels in a conscious way . . . we learn to realise that the gods are reminding us of all they created . . . things are coloured because the gods are speaking through them.

From 'Space Perspective to Colour Perspective', Dornach, 2 June 1923

COLOURS IN PLANTS

It is a question of discovering in the green of plants, what is the true quality, the essential nature of green.

The plant kingdom was formed during the previous metamorphosis of the earth, known as the Old Moon evolution, when there was no solid matter. This fluid state was permeated with flowing colour. Only on the surface did the fluid element begin to solidify. So it would be possible to say, looking back to this earlier stage of evolution, that in the formation of the plant we are concerned with an essential fluid condition in which green, as also colour generally, existed in flowing movement.

And it was only during the Earth period of evolution that the plants were able to take on a firm form and incorporate the mineral element. It became possible for the plant to have a definite and no longer fluctuating nature, so that what we now describe as the plant appears for the first time during Earth evolution. Only then could colour assume the character which we see in the plant today and appear as fixed green.

Green is not the only colour usually seen in a plant which, as we know, in the course of metamorphosis takes on other colours; it has yellow, blue or white flowers, or red flowers or fruit, as in the melon for instance, which is transformed from green to yellow. Quite a superficial observation shows us what happens when the plant takes on a colour other than green. When this happens you can quite easily observe that the appearance of these other colours is connected with the sun, with direct sunlight. Just consider how plants hide themselves and curl up if they cannot hold up their flowers to the sunlight. There is a connection, if only a superficial one, between the sun and certain parts of the plant not being coloured green. The sun, as it were, metamorphoses the green and transforms it.

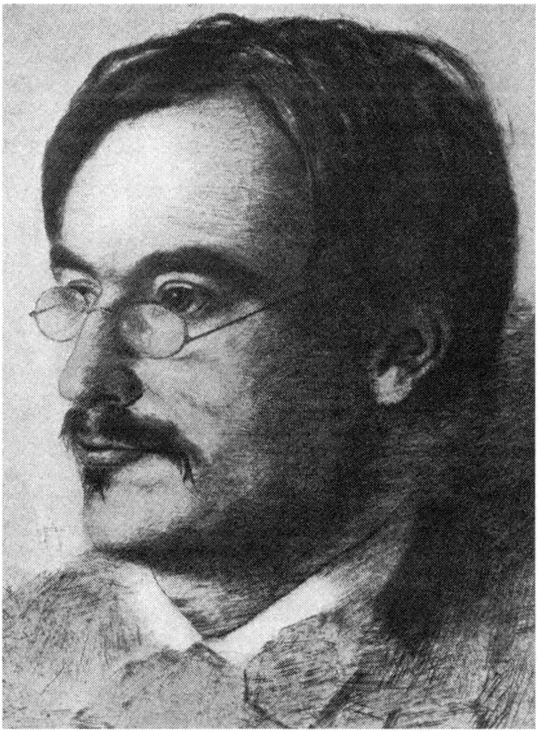

13. Rudolf Steiner, etching by Otto Fröhlich (c. 1891/92)

Here we can ask ourselves: what kind of heavenly body has the strongest effect on earth, working in an opposite way to the sun, to produce in the plant what the sunlight later metamorphoses, and transforms into other colours? What in fact causes green to arise within the plant kingdom?

We will be led to that heavenly body which appears as the polar opposite of the sun—the moon. Spiritual Science can establish the connection between the green of the plant and the moon and also between the other colours and the sun, by contrasting the properties of moonlight as opposed to sunlight, and especially by the way that moonlight works within sun-darkness. Thus in the plant we have an interplay of sun and moon influences. But at the same time we have an explanation of why green becomes an image and does not appear luminous in the plant as the other colours do. The other colours in the plant have a shining, lustre quality. If you observe the colours of flowers with the right kind of feeling you will see that they *shine* at you. Compare then with green: it is 'fixed' to the plant. You will see here nothing other than a copy of what you perceive in the cosmos. Sunlight shines: moonlight is the image of the sunlight. In the same way the image of light, colour as image, appears in the green of the plant. It is through the sun that lustre colours appear in the plant; the image colour, as something 'fixed', appears in green ...

But when we look at a plant in such a way that we know that cosmic forces are at work and that sun and moon forces interplay to produce colour in the plant, we have the basic elements for understanding how, with plants at least, colour is fixed in an object and becomes material. It is due to image, and not lustre, influences from the cosmos that colour becomes material. In the plant, green has become an image because the moon has been separated from the earth during the course of Earth evolution. In the separation of moon and earth we must seek the real origin of green in the plant kingdom. The plant is no longer exposed to moon-forces coming from within the earth but receives its image character from the cosmos.

In our feelings we comprehend the reciprocal relationships brought about by cosmic influences in the plant. We can therefore appreciate the character of green and the other colours in the plant through our sensitivity and through an artistic feeling for the nature of colour.

'Colour in Matter—Painting out of Colour', Dornach, 8 May 1921

There is no other sphere in which we experience a colour so intimately bound up with the inner nature of an object as green is with the plant.

From Spiritual Science you know that the plant owes its existence to the fact that, besides its physical body, it has an etheric body. It is the etheric body which is the source of life in the plant. But the etheric body is not green. What makes the plant green is to be found in its physical body . . . If the plant had no etheric body, it would be a mineral, and it is the mineral nature of the plant that appears as green. The etheric body is quite a different colour although it does reveal itself in the plant through the green of the mineral element.

'Colour Experience—Image Colours', Dornach, 6 May 1921

COLOUR IN ANIMALS

The element of colour is fundamentally flowing and alive and our soul lives in it. A time will come when we shall again recognize the living connection between the flowing world of colour and the coloured objects and creatures around us.

People find this difficult because, having to develop their ego during Earth-evolution, human beings have as it were ascended out of this flowing sea of colour to the level of clear self-awareness. With his ego man raises himself out of the flowing ocean of colour in which the animal world is still fully immersed, and if an animal has green, brown, red, black or white feathers or fur, it is because of its whole relationship to the flowing sea of colour. Just as we look at objects with our ego, an animal looks at them with his astral body, and into this astral body flow the forces of the animal's group soul.

Due to the kind of relationship that exists between an animal's astral body and the group soul, sensitivity to the living creativity of colour streams into an animal. And in the same way as our hand reaches out to take hold of an object we long to have, the animal's whole organism is affected by the living creativity of colour which flows straight in and colours its feathers or fur. As I have said before, the modern age cannot even grasp why a polar bear is white. The colour results from his environment, and the fact that he 'whitens' himself means the same thing, on a different level, as when a human being reaches out and picks a rose he craves for. The polar bear's life of instinct responds to the living creativity in his environment and he 'sucks in the white'.

'The Creative World of Colour', Dornach, 26 July 1914

BLACK

We can easily find something in nature which is just as characteristically black as the plant is green. We need only look at carbon. If we remember that carbon can also become quite clear and transparent—indeed, a diamond—we will be able to understand this connection of blackness with carbon most clearly. For black is so characteristic of carbon that, were it not black but white and transparent, it would be a diamond. Black is so integral a part of carbon, that the latter really owes its whole existence to the blackness. Carbon really finds its own nature in the blackness, the darkness, in which it appears. Just as the plant has its image in green, so does carbon have its image in black.

Now submerge yourself in black; you are completely surrounded by black—in this black darkness a physical being can do nothing. Life is driven out of the plant when it becomes carbon. Black shows itself alien to life, hostile to life; when plants are carbonized they turn black. Life, then, can do nothing in blackness. And the soul? Our soul life deserts us when this awful blackness is within us. But the spirit flourishes; the spirit can penetrate the blackness and assert itself within it.

'Colour Experience—Image Colours', from: *Colour*, Dornach, 6 May 1921

WHITE

White cannot be said to be the characteristic colour of any being in the outer world. We could turn to the mineral kingdom, but it would be better to look in quite another direction to form an objective idea of the colour white.

Let us imagine that we have some white, (a white surface) in front of us, and light plays upon it, illuminating it. At once we feel a certain kinship between the white and the light.

At first this is merely an impression, but it becomes more than an impression the moment we turn to the sun itself. For the sun has a certain whiteness in its light.

In order to understand white we should let ourselves be led by white to the light as such. In order to strengthen this feeling, we need only remember that the opposite of white is black. We have no doubt that black is darkness; we can very easily identify white with brightness, with the light as such. In short, we find an inner connection between light and white when we allow our feelings to speak to us . . . When we wake in the morning and the light streams around and through us, we become inwardly aware of ourselves; we feel an inner kinship between the light and our own essential being. At night, if we wake up in dense darkness, we feel we cannot reach our real being; we have returned to some extent to ourselves but under such conditions we do not feel in our true element. And we know, too, that what we receive from the light is a 'coming to ourselves'. There is no contradiction in the fact that the blind are without this experience; the point is that their organism is designed for it.

We have the same relationship to light that our 'I' has to the world; yet not quite the same, since we cannot say that because the light fills us we gain our 'I'. Nevertheless, for us to gain this 'I', light is essential if we are beings with sight.

What underlies this fact? In light, which we have said is represented by white—we have still to learn the inner connection between the two—we find what really fills us with spirit, connects us with our own spirit. There is a definite connection between the 'I', our spiritual being, and the experience of light shining through us.

'Colour Experience—Image Colours', Dornach, 6 May 1921

YELLOW

If we are painting, let us take yellow in its essential, inner quality and attempt to spread it on a surface. You will see that a yellow surface with definite boundaries is a repulsive thing; it is quite unbearable to artistic feeling. The soul cannot bear a yellow surface which is limited. We must make yellow paler at the edges, then paler still; in short, the yellow must be full in the centre, shining out into a still paler yellow. If we are to experience its inner nature we cannot imagine yellow in any other way. Yellow must shine outwards.

It must be deeper in the centre and radiate; it must spread out, becoming less concentrated and weaker all the time. This is what I might call the secret of yellow. It is like mocking the very nature of yellow to give it a boundary, which is something imposed by man. Yellow is gagged when it is confined, for it does not want to be bounded but to radiate in all directions.

Yellow radiates outwardly, it shines, and is luminous. It can make us feel joyful. Through yellow we can become more attuned to our own 'I'—we are filled with spirit. Yellow, shining into you as spirit, becomes the lustre of the spirit.

'Lustre and Image', Dornach, 7 May 1921

If we unite ourselves with a yellow surface we feel as though we were transported back to the beginning of our cycle of time. We feel that we are then living in the forces out of which we were created when we entered upon our first earthly incarnation. You feel an affinity between what you are throughout the whole of Earth existence and what comes to meet you from the world into which you take the yellow with which you are united.

'Moral Experience of the Worlds of Colour and Tone', Dornach, 1 January 1915

RED

We will simply imagine that we are looking at a surface shining all over with the same shade of strong vermilion. And let us assume we succeed in forgetting everything else around us and concentrate entirely on experiencing this colour, so that we have the colour in front of us—not merely as something that works upon us but as something with which we ourselves are united, that we are within. You will then be able to feel as though you were in the world, and in this world the whole of you has become colour, the whole of our innermost soul, and wherever your soul goes in the world you will be a soul filled with red—living in, with, and out of red. Yet you will not be able to experience this intensely in the soul unless the corresponding feeling is transformed into moral experience, real moral experience.

If we swim through the world as though we were red, had identified ourselves with red, and our very soul and the whole world were entirely red, we shall not be able to help feeling that this whole red world is filling us with the substance of divine wrath, coming towards us from all sides in response to all the possibilities of evil and sin in us. In this infinite red space we shall be able to feel as though we were before the judgment of God, and our moral feeling will become the kind of moral experience our souls can have in infinite space. And when the reaction comes, when something emerges in our soul as we are having this experience in infinite red—or, I could also say in the one and only red—I can only describe it by saying we learn to pray. If you can experience the raying and glowing of divine wrath, together with all the possibilities of evil in the human soul, and if you can experience in the red how one learns to pray, the experience of red is enormously deepened. We can also experience the form red takes on when it enters space.

We can then understand how we can experience a being that radiates goodness and is full of divine kindness and mercy, a being that we want to feel in the realm of space. Then we shall feel the need to express this divine mercy and goodness in a form which arises out of the colour itself. We shall feel the need to let space be pushed aside so that goodness and mercy may shine forth. Before space was there it was all concentrated at the centre, and now goodness and mercy enter space and, just as clouds are driven apart, space is rent asunder and recedes to make way for mercy, and we have the feeling that what is being scattered must be drawn in red. Here in the centre we shall have to indicate faintly a kind of magenta shining into the scattering red.

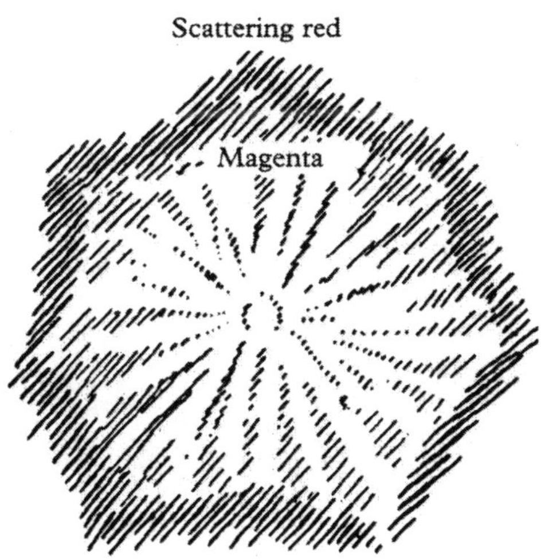

We shall then be present with our whole soul as the colour takes on form. And with our whole soul we shall feel an echo of how the beings who belong especially to our Earth process felt when they had ascended to the Elohim stage and learnt to fashion the world of forms out of colours. We shall learn to experience something of the creative activity of the Spirits of Form, who are the Elohim, and we shall then understand how colour can create forms.

'Moral Experience and the Worlds of Colour and Tone', Dornach, 1 January 1915

BLUE

Blue shines inwards, towards itself. If we are painting blue, we paint it fuller and deeper on the outside edge and weaker, or paler, in the middle. Blue gathers itself up at the edges, flowing together in a wave which gathers around a lighter blue in the centre. Blue must be painted so that it can withdraw, as it were, into itself.

Blue, gathering itself together inwardly, enclosed within itself, is the lustre of the soul.

'Lustre and Image', Dornach, 7 May 1921

If you identify yourself entirely with a blue surface you would go through the world with the desire to accompany the blue forever and to overcome your egotism—become macrocosmic, as it were—and develop devotion. And you would find it a blessing if you could remain like this for your meeting with divine mercy. You would feel blessed by divine mercy if you could go through the world like this.

'Moral Experience of the Worlds of Colour and Tone', Dornach, 1 January 1915

. . . Angels bore light into the darkness, and darkness into the light. They became the mediators and messengers between light and darkness. And what had previously only shone in the light and brought its shadow, the airy darkness, after it, now burst into colour, changing from one colour to another, as the light appeared in the darkness and the darkness in the light. It is the third Hierarchy, the Angels, Archai and Archangels, who created colours out of light and darkness.

'The Hierarchies and the Nature of the Rainbow', Dornach, 4 January 1924

Bibliography

Quotations from Aristotle:

Minor Works, Chapter 'On Colour' (*De Coloribus*). Transl. W. H. Hett. Pub. Leob Classical Library, Cambridge, Mass., 1980

Complete Works, Ed. J. A. Smith and W. D. Ross, 12 Vols., Oxford 1908-52. Revised ed. by J. Barnes, 2 Vols. Princeton, N.J., 1984

Further Reading:

Aristotle, W. Ross, London, 1923

Aristotle the Philosopher, J. L. Ackvill, Oxford, 1981

Aristotle's Theory of Poetry and Fine Art, S. H. Butler, Publ. Dover, 1951

Essays on the History of Aesthetics, Ed. by Peter Kiy, Chapter 'Art and Nature in Classical Philosophy' by A. J. Close. Publ. Univ. of Rochester Press

The Oxford Dictionary of the Christian Church. Ref. Aristotle. Publ. Oxford Univ. Press

Philosophies of Art and Beauty—Selected Readings in Aesthetics from Plato to Heidegger, Ed. Albert Hofstadter and Richard Kuhns, Publ. Univ. Chicago Press, 1964

Quotations from Thomas Aquinas:

Summa Theologica, 60 Vols. plus Index. Blackfriars Publ. London, 1964–81

Further Reading:

The Philosophy of Thomas Aquinas, Rudolf Steiner, 3 Lectures: 'The Essence of Thomism', 'The Application of Intelligence', 'Man as a Learning Being', 1920, Dornach. Publ. Percy Lund, Humphries & Co. Ltd., London, 1932

The Great Scientists, Jack Meadows, Oxford Univ. Press, 1986

Art and Beauty in the Middle Ages, Umberto Eco, Yale Univ. Press, 1986

Quotations from Rudolf Steiner:

The Arts and Their Mission, Publ. Anthroposophic Press, Spring Valley, New York, 1964

Art as Seen in the Light of Mystery Wisdom, Publ. Rudolf Steiner Press, London/Sussex, 1986

Colour, Twelve Lectures by Rudolf Steiner. Publ. Rudolf Steiner Press, 1971

Further Reading:

The Individuality of Colour, E. Koch/G. Wagner, Publ. Rudolf Steiner Press, Sussex, 2009

Art Inspired by Rudolf Steiner, John Fletcher, Publ. Mercury Arts, 1987

The Language of Colour in the First Goetheanum, Hilde Raske. Publ. Walter Keller Verlag, Dornach, 1983

Architecture as a Synthesis of the Arts, Lectures by Rudolf Steiner. Publ. Rudolf Steiner Press, London/Sussex, 1999

A note from the publisher

For more than a quarter of a century, **Temple Lodge Publishing** has made available new thought, ideas and research in the field of spiritual science.

Anthroposophy, as founded by Rudolf Steiner (1861-1925), is commonly known today through its practical applications, principally in education (Steiner-Waldorf schools) and agriculture (biodynamic food and wine). But behind this outer activity stands the core discipline of spiritual science, which continues to be developed and updated. True science can never be static and anthroposophy is living knowledge.

Our list features some of the best contemporary spiritual-scientific work available today, as well as introductory titles. So, visit us online at **www.templelodge.com** and join our emailing list for news on new titles.

If you feel like supporting our work, you can do so by buying our books or making a direct donation (we are a non-profit/ charitable organisation).